Narratives That Change Minds

Narratives That Change Minds

Technical Communication of Risk, Crisis, and Change

Dirk Remley

BEP

BUSINESS EXPERT PRESS

Leader in applied, concise business books

Narratives that Change Minds:
Technical Communication of Risk, Crisis, and Change

Copyright © Business Expert Press, LLC, 2026.

Cover design by Cassandra Kronstedt

Interior design by S4Carlisle Publishing Services, Chennai, India

First published in 2025 by
Business Expert Press, LLC
222 East 46th Street, New York, NY 10017
www.businessexpertpress.com

ISBN-13: 978-1-63742-910-5 (paperback)
ISBN-13: 978-1-63742-911-2 (e-book)

Corporate Communications Collection

First edition: 2025

10 9 8 7 6 5 4 3 2 1

EU SAFETY REPRESENTATIVE
Mare Nostrum Group B.V.
Mauritskade 21D
1091 GC Amsterdam
The Netherlands
gpsr@mare-nostrum.co.uk

Description

Among the most challenging tasks any leader faces are communicating to various audiences how to change behaviors to limit risks, address crises, and change the way an organization operates—especially as they relate to scientific and technical issues. Executives, managers, and officials deal with multiple audiences—employees, boards, and the public—who may have competing perspectives or lack an understanding of technical or scientific issues affecting them. This book provides a framework for analysis and case studies of leadership successes and failures relative to communicating risk, crisis, and organizational change. The goal is to help managers and executives understand how to incorporate narrative as they communicate with various audiences to improve the likelihood of facilitating needed change. A unique feature of this book is its consideration of neuroscience elements that affect how audiences respond to messages.

We will explore the *why*s and *how*s of effects multiple forms of communication have on individuals, drawing on scholarship about how the brain processes information from different stimuli and experiences. The book includes a practical model that provides guidance to executives and managers—whether they have technical background in their field or come from a managerial background—in effectively applying principles valued in leadership development programming. Case studies of narratives from technical fields including safety engineering in aeronautics, automotive manufacturing, health care, artificial intelligence, and specialized financial contexts, among others, help illustrate application of the model. This unique approach makes the book an excellent addition to reading lists of leadership development and communication programs.

Contents

List of Figures

Acknowledgments

I thank my colleagues who provided feedback toward improving drafts of this work. Listed in order of which I received their feedback:

Christa Teston, Professor of English at the Ohio State University, who directs Business and Technical Writing and the college's Reader Experience Lab—particularly for her background in medical rhetoric and medical humanities.

Derek Van Ittersum, Professor of English at Kent State University—particularly for his expertise with multimodal and digital composing and narratives associated with technical communication.

Katie Robisch, Lecturer of English at Case Western Reserve University, who teaches courses in professional communication for engineers, technical communication, and writing in the health professions.

Also, I thank Collection Editor Debbie DuFrene for her suggestions toward refining the phrasing and clarity of the content.

Prologue

A man is nearing retirement age, and he wants to know the risks of a limited income and a lot of time on one's hands and how to avoid or limit them. He does an online search of the term "risks in retirement planning," and he finds several sites identifying various risks. He wants to know more about risks and specific experiences with them. He has a former colleague who retired a few years before; so, he seeks out that person's counsel. That person shares stories of a couple of personal health crises that had some economic impacts in his first two years of retirement and, also, how he volunteered at a local organization and made a few new friends there.

A woman who is pregnant for the first time has looked at many books and websites acknowledging what to expect in the first year of mother-hood. Still, she wants to know more about specific experiences and what she can expect more personally. She asks her friends who have already started families about what to expect in the first year of being a mother to prepare for her new life of motherhood. They respond with their own experiences—personal narratives of how their life was in the first days, weeks, and months after their child's birth. A couple of them describe a financial crisis they dealt with because their husband lost his job, or the baby had an illness that lasted longer than expected; another describes almost leaving their newborn in the car when going shopping because she had not yet adjusted to the routine of bringing the baby along.

A high school student thinking about a career that involves working with chemicals has explored a number of websites that describe the career. However, the student wants to learn about the daily activity of a professional in the field and how potential hazards are addressed, and they have the opportunity to seek information from a professional in that field who is the friend of a relative. That person responds with a story about precautions his workplace takes and shares a story about a recent safety crisis associated with a project at work.

A fifth-grade boy is about to get a vaccination required for school, and he is nervous, not knowing what to expect. His parents and other adults reassure him that it will only feel like a small "prick" and not hurt much or for very long. Nevertheless, he has a friend who had the shot the week before, and he asks the friend directly about her experience—what it is like, and how long it hurt. The friend responds that it was like being poked with a stick and, afterward, like the dull pain of being lightly punched in the arm, lasting a few seconds.

None of these examples offers highly technical information. I share them to note common elements between the kinds of stories we seek out or share with friends and relatives on a regular basis and narratives found in highly technical contexts relative to what to do when some risk or crisis is involved—either of which involves some degree of changing behavior. The common thread among these scenarios is that general information—facts, data, statistics—about each "question" is readily available online; yet, the person seeks out stories that provide details of relevant experience beyond that general information, and they are provided by trusted people: people with relevant experience, people the person knows or understands to have expertise, one who can relate to the person asking the question, and people who are like the person asking the question. In each case, the person seeking information seeks specific details to help them understand what to expect in terms of risks, crises, or outright change in life and how they might respond to related situations.

The stories provide information about human experience not included in technical or scientific data or statistics. Such data and statistics are important to understanding a phenomenon generally and may be part of the narrative, but people want to know the stories of how individuals or families were affected and how they dealt with risk, crisis, and change. People can relate to those stories more than they can relate to data.

Further, the use of technical jargon in describing an event is fine when the audience fully understands that terminology; however, it hinders an audience's ability not only to understand the situation but why they should act on any suggestions to limit risk or potential crises. A description of symptoms of a problem or behaviors that will help reduce exposure to risk or crisis or a description of how people adjusted when facing a similar situation helps audiences better understand how they might behave.

Relating to people is a challenge when communicating information about scientific or technical-related risks, crises, and outright change to employees, supervisors, or the general public. It is easier to cite data about the risk, how to address the issue, or the chances of success with change. Yet, humans want to hear how specific people like them succeeded with similar changes in behavior under similar circumstances. Those stories offer hope. Even stories involving negative outcomes are valued, because they help people understand what to avoid as they try to address a problem. This book addresses the importance of stories when communicating with others about risk, crisis, and change associated with technical and scientific issues. I expand on the above narratives with two of my own. Each is based on an "everyday activity." That is, people may do them on a regular basis; they are not rare situations. Further, each involves some technical elements that most people who participate in the activities know about through their own experiences or having learned about them from others. I use them to show how elements of narratives about risks and crises associated with everyday activities can relate to narratives about more technically involved contexts.

Riding My Bicycle

I try to exercise regularly. I take regular walks, weather-permitting, usually two miles each day. I also enjoy riding my bicycle for exercise, weather-permitting; however, I do not take leisurely rides. Indeed, I use the ride as a cardiovascular workout. My bicycle route is 20 miles each trip, and most of it is done on a bike/hike trail that is asphalt. It involves a round-trip on the entirety of the trail; so, I pass particular points/areas on the trail twice on my ride. The bike/hike trail is owned and operated by the county parks district. Generally, I use the higher gears throughout the ride, including a few relatively steep or lengthy inclines. Typically, it takes me about 70 to 75 minutes to complete the ride, which means that I average about 16 to 17 miles per hour.

During riding season (generally mid-May to late-September or early-October), I ride on weekends and holidays, days on which most get a day off from work. This reduces the risks associated with riding on streets and crossing streets along the trail. There are several risks associated with riding a bicycle as I do, and I take action to reduce the likelihood of those risks occurring. I think about what I can do to minimize risks, and I communicate decisions implicitly to myself. Occasionally, I experience a crisis on the ride—something that is short-lived but that forces me to change some aspect of my usual ride. I have to think about how to change my behavior, usually on short notice; and I communicate that change "on the fly." I have, also, had to change the route entirely in order to continue the goal of a 20-mile ride. That generally takes longer to think about, research, and implement. One can find general information about such risks online, but the actual experiences I've had provide different insights to guide action.

I am using the example of my bicycle rides to illustrate narratives of change associated with risk, crisis, and outright change in operation. Most people either ride a bicycle, know someone who rides, or encounters bicyclists as they drive their own vehicle on roads periodically. So, this acts as a way to help readers understand various concepts I present throughout this book. I use it also because it is a narrative, and narratives help to facilitate change by engaging audience's attention effectively. People like hearing stories. There are multiple reasons for that. Stories represent a concrete reality linking human experience to complex phenomena. Stories engage neural elements that help audience understand complex concepts and how they might relate to them in their own reality. Let's consider some additional details about each of the scenarios I mentioned in the previous paragraph to advance an understanding of phenomena associated with risk, crisis, and change and how to communicate changes related to each. Because it is a personal narrative, I consider how I communicated each change to myself and what helped me accept those decisions.

Risk

I mentioned that there are several risks involved in my bicycle rides and that I take certain actions to minimize their chances of occurring. Generally, the risk involved is that I may be injured, or my bicycle damaged at some point because of something outside of my control. Let us consider these risks. They include:

a. encountering motor vehicles in various locations along the route that I use, resulting in an accident and damage to me and/or my bicycle;

b. encountering potholes or ruts in the asphalt along the pavement on the route, resulting in damage to my bicycle or a fall off of my bicycle;

c. encountering people—either riding their own bicycle or walking, with others or alone—who may impede my ride or with whom I may collide;

d. encountering animals—wild or domestic—who may bite.

These are not unique to me and my route; all bicyclists face these kinds of risks and take appropriate action to reduce the chances of their occurrence. They are not technical or scientific issues either; however, there is specialized knowledge about them and how to address them that bicyclists develop with experience.

To reduce most of the listed risks, I tend to take my rides on weekends, when there is much less traffic on roads. Of course, I wear a helmet as a safety precaution. There is still traffic, but the risk of a vehicle hitting me is reduced dramatically than if I were riding during a weekday. Further reducing this risk, I tend to take my ride early in the morning, usually starting around 6:30 am. There are not many people on the road at that time, the sun has risen, I can see the road clearly, and people driving motor vehicles can clearly see me. A crisis may occur if I come upon a motor vehicle as I am turning onto or off the trail or when crossing any of the intersections where the trail is interrupted by a street. However, this is addressed by slowing down as I approach these areas or stopping if a vehicle appears. Similarly, reducing other risks involves merely slowing down and navigating carefully.

Crises and Change

Let's now consider one specific episode that I experienced on my usual ride that required changes in behavior. It involved a slowly increasing risk that rose to the need for a significant change in behavior. I include some elements of cognition and emotional response that came into play to exhibit some neuroscientific dynamics within such cases and what would be involved in communicating related changes.

Riding on Ruts

Ruts, or buckling of the asphalt, develop over time. As time passes and small ruts become larger or more ruts develop, they become a risk. In my experience, ruts developed unaddressed over a period of three to four years to the point that I had to change my route to attain my goal of the 20-mile ride. These small, raised cracks in the asphalt create bumps that one must either ride over or try to avoid by swerving to either side of the trail to avoid hitting them. Swerving creates additional work and hazard, especially if any other people are on the trail in that area. Hitting a rut when riding a rigid framed bicycle is very uncomfortable and creates stress on muscles.

Most of the rutted areas are short (a few yards long), and the ruts are relatively small. They are easily avoided or small enough not to risk damage to the bicycle. However, in one section of the trail, near its west end, the ruts grew to the point that I could not ride that section without worrying about damaging my bicycle or risking injury to myself. The section is about a quarter of a mile long, and there were *several* ruts on both sides of the trail. For about three years, I noticed the ruts developing, and I usually rode on the south side of the trail in either direction—that side had fewer and smaller ruts. However, on my first weekend of riding one season, I noticed that both sides were in bad shape, and I decided to change the route to avoid that strip.

As I rode that first weekend, I made the decision not to ride that portion until it was repaired. This represented a genuine, longer-term change in course. Before the next weekend of riding, I did some research to ascertain where I could make up the "lost" half-mile (again, the strip is about one-quarter mile long, and I would ride it twice—out and back—each day). I found a section of the road that I use as my turn-around at the east end of the trail to use to make that up. So, I was still able to complete the goal of a 20-mile ride.

The adjustment was relatively easy for me to make. I was *motivated* to maintain the length of the ride, so I put forth a good effort to locate an alternative. The change I made was *minimal and fluid*; just adding a little more beyond the end of the trail portion. Also, I was *familiar* with the road that I used to replace the "lost" quarter mile. Before the trail was completed, I used that road for most of my previous route; I had used a portion of the uncompleted trail to access that road. It is a rural road that does not have much traffic on weekends. So, while I understood that the road brought with it new risk—motor vehicle traffic (and near a truck port), I would be on it for a short period—only half a mile, and there would be minimal traffic.

This route change worked out well for certain reasons that are detailed in this book, among them the italicized terms. I share another story about a difficult experience that I had on a golf course and that links more closely with the technical nature of this book. I use it to demonstrate further the importance of shared experiences in understanding potential risks and crises toward modifying behavior accordingly and that the absence of certain information and experiences that were included in the previous story contributed to my failure to adjust to an evolving medical crisis. That is, while I had considerable experience with bicycling situations and could make a change relatively easily to address a risk in that setting, the next case involves my lack of knowledge and experience with a not uncommon medical condition. Had I had previous experience or someone had shared a narrative about their own experience with the situation, I would have understood what to do.

A Golf Outing Gone Bad

Long ago, I used to golf somewhat regularly—mostly on weekends. Almost always I would golf with friends or relatives. Usually, I would take a walking cart because it is much less expensive to buy or rent a walking cart than to rent a riding cart. Sometimes I would take a riding cart, especially if there were several groups golfing that day and the pace needed to move more quickly. When I was in my twenties, sometimes, I would carry my bag myself; I was young and healthy.

One particular golf outing did not go well, as I wound up ending my round early due to a medical crisis. It was a very hot summer day, and I had been walking the course. Over a series of the middle four or five holes, I noticed several "symptoms" associated with my declining condition; however, I did not understand what they were because I had never experienced them or heard anyone talk about their own experience with them. I had no training to help me understand how serious the situation was becoming. I had heard of the terms "heat exhaustion" and "heat stroke," but I had no experience or real understanding of them beyond the concepts of excessive sweating and muscle cramping. While my experiences and awareness of the various risks and potential crises associated with bicycling helped me move through each issue, my lack of awareness about heat-related conditions negatively affected my ability to manage them. Indeed, it was not until a few days after the outing that I came to understand what I had experienced and its seriousness.

The story of the outing needs to begin with the night before the outing. It was a hot night—the low was between 70 and 72 degrees (F). Further, I had stayed with one of the friends with whom I was golfing the next day, so as to avoid a long, early drive. His house did not have air conditioning or even a fan. While I sought some relief from a cold, wet face rag, I did not sleep well because of the heat and sweating throughout the night. The morning of the outing, that friend and I met a third person at a restaurant for breakfast. I took all kinds of liquids, knowing that I needed to hydrate; it would be another hot day. The high was expected to be in the low 90s. I had tea, milk, and juice with an otherwise healthy breakfast.

The three of us made our way to the golf course and began our round—18 holes—around mid-morning. The temperature was already in the 80s (degrees F), and I noticed that a water station had been set up at almost every tee area. I took water at each as I moved through each hole. As I could anticipate, I was sweating quite a bit by the fifth hole, wiping sweat from my face and arms with almost each shot. I had experienced that before, so I was not concerned. I just made sure to continue taking water at each tee area. However, things took a turn into new territory around the eighth hole.

We moved from the seventh green to the tee area of the eighth hole, which was backed up a bit. I went to pour myself some water from the water station, and I noticed that there was no sweat on my arms—at all. My arms were completely dry, red, and hot to the touch. I recall finding that interesting at the time, but that was all. I was taking water at a good rate. Surely, I had been hydrating well. Nevertheless, I was very hot, and I was taking a bit longer to walk to each shot on each hole.

I recall walking down the ninth hole with a slower gait, my leg muscles were tightening up and cramping, my body felt very hot, and my skin looked red. By the time we "made the turn" to the back nine holes, not only was I moving more slowly and not sweating, but it was becoming increasingly more difficult to swing... and breathe.

As I walked the tenth hole, trouble became even more apparent. I knew my swing was becoming weaker; so, I adjusted by taking longer clubs on the fairway to compensate for the weaker swing. Still, I was struggling to swing with much energy, and my gait was down to a trudge. It felt like I was somehow dragging myself as well as my bag down the fairway and through the green. The story becomes a bit vague at this point, but my memory of being very disoriented remains.

I do not know on which hole I stopped my round. I recall a period of moving almost mechanically. My recollection of the hole's design is that of the eleventh hole according to the course's layout online. There was a portion of a small pond jutting onto the left side of the fairway on that hole, short of what a reasonable tee shot would be for most. The right side of the fairway was clear, but I had lost some control of my shots. Because my swings had become so weak, I knew I needed more effort than I would otherwise have needed to clear that piece of water if my ball happened to go to the left. I gave it all that I had.

My shot made it to the right side of the fairway beyond the water hazard—actually a pretty good shot considering. I trudged, gasped for breath, and almost limped to my ball, my legs so tight. As I came upon my ball and assessed the situation, I looked to my friends and declared that I could not go on. I picked up my ball and headed for the clubhouse. However, locating the clubhouse was a challenge; I was entirely disoriented.

As the hole was the eleventh, the clubhouse was a relatively short distance away, straight through a wooded area. However, given my confusion and disoriented state, it was a challenge; I recall walking around like a lost hiker without a compass, finally finding the clubhouse after what seemed like at least half a mile. Not realizing the severity of my situation, instead of going into the clubhouse for some attention, I sat at a table under a canopy and waited for my friends to finish. Eventually, I made it back home, and I went straight to the shower for relief and sat in the shower for several minutes under cool to cold water. I would struggle to walk for the next week as I recovered, my leg muscles very tight. Figuring that I just had a bad experience and would recover after a couple of days, I did not seek medical attention at all.

At home, I had a medical book that provided a lot of information about different kinds of illnesses, conditions, and surgeries (this was just before the Internet was easily available). With each condition, it listed symptoms, then detailed what physiological elements the condition involved, and what treatment might include—always encouraging the reader to consult with a medical professional to ascertain specific treatment. At some point during that week, I looked into the book to see what was going on. I immediately turned to information about heat exhaustion, because I was aware that some athletes experienced that in hot weather; it's a risk associated with outdoor activities that many athletes are aware of. I had never experienced it or heard much other than an athlete stopping to rehydrate and then resuming activity. Maybe I had now experienced it. The listing of symptoms included body temperature data—I did not have a thermometer with me at the time (nor would I expect anyone to have one with them wherever they go); so, that information was useless to me. However, the listing also included several other physical attributes characteristic of the condition and with which I could compare to my own experience.

As I went through the listing of symptoms of heat exhaustion, I realized that my condition had gone beyond that. Fortunately, right next to the listing for heat exhaustion was that for heat stroke, which is less common than heat exhaustion but not uncommon. I had experienced several of those symptoms. As I looked more into heat stroke, I came to understand that I had not only experienced heat stroke but that I was very near to having a severe medical emergency. Each symptom suggests that some part of the body is at a stage of shutting down, and prolonged exposure and delayed treatment can result in death. Having never experienced heat stroke or known anyone who did, I did not understand that I was experiencing a medical crisis or how to change my behavior appropriately to respond to it. The only change in my behavior was to stop golfing and wait for my friends.

While the information in the medical book included body temperature, it was the physical characteristics of the condition that were most relevant to me as explored what I experienced. Had I gone into the clubhouse to let staff there know of my struggles, they probably would have been able to help, trained to recognize and treat (at least initially) the symptoms. As professionals of the golf community, they probably knew people who have experienced heat exhaustion and heat stroke. The friends with whom I was golfing probably had never experienced the condition either, and so, they did not understand that I was struggling.

Prologue Conclusion

I have included these narratives to illustrate a few dynamics associated with risk, crisis, and long-term change and how management might effectively communicate them. Compare the two sets of stories— riding a bicycle and the golf outing. Note that with each element in the bicycle-riding narrative, I called attention to previous experiences that helped me facilitate change in my behaviors, and I mentioned emotional responses affecting how I perceived a situation. Also, notice that the golf outing narrative involves lack of awareness of several attributes of medical conditions, partly due to my own lack of training and partly because I had no experience with it before or knew anyone who had shared a similar story with me. I was entirely unable to adapt because I had no reference point. Within technical and scientific settings, the narratives of previous experiences with similar situations helps to inform how we can change our behavior to address such risks and crises.

Throughout the book, I will refer to some elements of these narratives to help the reader recall points while making neuroscientific connections to those attributes. They also help to identify a rubric or model that we can use to help design effective messages.

CHAPTER 1

Introduction

We are always aware of the risks of clicking on a mysterious popup or notification when we are on our computer, especially if we are online. Such popups/notifications might involve malware that can wreak havoc on our computer. A single item can infect a file or the entire computer with a virus. If we use a jump drive to transport files to other computers, the files and systems on that computer can become infected as well. If a network is involved, the entire network may become infected, sharing the virus or other malware with others who use the network.

In spite of such awareness, I have sometimes clicked on such popups/notifications and experienced these issues. They are more than an inconvenience, because, as they spread, they create a crisis for all who encounter the effects. One such experience involved my entire jump drive becoming infected such that I could not open or use any files; I had to reformat the jump drive and lost all the files on it. In that same episode, before I discovered the infection, I had used the drive on another computer that was part of a network. As I became aware of the virus on my drive, I alerted the network administrator about the potential infection to the network. I described what I did, what machines I used, and what was happening with my own files. Since I had used machines on the particular network before experiencing symptoms of the infection, those machines could be infected. The network administrator quickly dropped what she was doing to investigate. Sure enough, the network was infected. It took them most of the morning to clean the system and then put out an announcement for others who may have used computers in that system to check their jump drives.

In another, different incident, the IT people at my institution shut down my account, acknowledging that it had been compromised. Unaware of any malware exposure and curious, I inquired about what had happened. Evidently, an email message that I had received that was related to the institution's Learning Management System (LMS) and that I had clicked on turned out to be malicious. The particular URL address had an extension that looked like it was linked to a reputable institution with which I understood there was a relationship with the LMS. The IT people explained sympathetically that a more careful reading of the URL showed a subtle difference that many would not pick up. The IT people were aware of this malware risk, and they eventually announced it to the university community; I had not been the only one exposed to it.

Fortunately, in each case, IT people were able to manage the situation; they were trained to handle such incidents. With each case, the narrative of the risk emerged after the risk event took place—exposure to malware had occurred. A description of the event emerged to inform future action; this is *descriptive narrative*: narrative that describes something that happened, provides some reflection on causes, and suggests possible future action.

With each similar experience, I grew wiser about these risks and reviewed information about how to limit or avoid them. In many of these cases, the information I reviewed offered *evaluative narratives*: narratives of events that happened, critique of the actions of those involved and their actions to address it, and evaluation of my own actions. As suggested, these may have started as descriptive narratives from my own or others' experiences, and I used them in a process to evaluate what to do to respond to a risky situation before taking action.

Relatively recently (early 2025), in fact, I experienced popup notifications encouraging me to update my security software by purchasing new software. It was on the university-issued laptop, and, consequently, I figured that any updates would be automatic, and I would not have to pay for them. I did not click on these popups and alerted the department's IT person, explaining, as I had done in previous such experiences, what happened. He was able to locate a malicious file that affected my web browser. Again, his technical training helped to address the problem, and my technical background with such phenomena helped to avoid the risk from becoming a crisis for me. My own experiences and information I had seen about how to address the potential risks acted as *prescriptive narratives* for me. They explained what action I should take to prevent the risky event. These may have started as descriptive narratives of previous experiences, were eventually used to evaluate a course of action one could take to avoid the risk or crisis in a similar situation, and identify a specific set of steps to take in that situation to reduce or eliminate the risk or crisis.

All of these cases have three things in common:

- the issue involved an existing risk that could (or did) grow into a crisis;
- the issue was technical in nature and needed someone with technical training to address it;
- a detailed explanation of what happened and awareness of how to address it through shared experiences of similar incidents facilitated adjustment to reduce further risk or avoid further crisis.

Understanding how all of these elements work together—whether one-on-one or in a larger, organizational setting—is important. It is through such interactions that people become aware of potential risks and how to address them before they become bigger issues, or, as they become bigger issues, how to address them before they become too big. In some cases, a crisis may involve a need to change something in an organized system, bringing about its own concerns since change is generally recognized as stressful. Yet, these same ways we communicate potential risks so others can limit exposure or address crises help navigate change as well.

Effective communication is essential when addressing the most challenging of situations organizational and public leaders face: risk, crisis, and change. Broadly defined, risk communication identifies potential risks associated with a product, event, or activity (such as risk of a head injury when playing football); crisis communication seeks to respond to the negative impact of an event that may happen, is happening, or has happened (such as the COVID-19 public health crisis), and change communication conveys how an organization is changing its approach to the economic or operating environment (such as shifting to electric vehicles or changing what has been identified as a toxic culture, responding to economic pressures), or changing a process due to safety concerns.

While each challenge can be considered as separate situations with accompanying communication strategies, they may be integrated into any combination or sequence: a single accident or incident identifying a risk within a certain task or process, risk leading into crisis, crisis leading to change, or risk evolving into crisis and requiring change. Indeed, Angeli states, "[i]n technical and professional communication, scholars have tended more fully to risk communication instead of crisis communication. Our contributions to crisis communication subsume 'crisis' under 'risk'...."[1] Crises affecting large numbers of people or an organization often begin with the identification of a risk that subsequently grows.

In recent years, several events involving risks, crises, and change have required the use of specialized terminology and other complex communication considerations. Because these events included technical and scientific concepts, those organizational leaders and public officials communicating the message had to consider that their various audiences may not fully understand the issues. Consequently, they had to apply several attributes of technical communication. Particularly in technical settings, there are multiple audiences: those employees internal to the organization or field and its workings to external audiences—oftentimes, the general public—that have very little awareness of internal operations and technical details associated with the subject matter. Further, those in positions of leadership needed to listen carefully to experts connected to the risk or crisis to understand details and make decisions about how to address them. Those technical experts needed to be able to communicate with decision-makers.

Indeed, the COVID-19 situation of 2020 to 2022 involved many organizations engaging in risk, crisis, and change and the accompanying challenges with communication. Early on, the U.S. federal and state governments had to assess the potential public health risks and implications related to the spread of COVID-19 virus as cases emerged in other countries and began spreading in the United States. By February 2020, most communication was that there was evidence of COVID but not understanding how quickly it could spread and how strong it was. The situation for governments became a crisis when the virus spread at such a rate that by March 2020, hospitals were struggling to keep pace with patients admitted for treatment. In response to the crisis, governments began shutting down what it deemed "nonessential" businesses and implementing mask mandates in various public settings, with varying degrees of effectiveness. As COVID-19 vaccines were developed, governments implemented vaccine mandates while allowing some businesses to reopen. Once vaccines were made available to a majority of the general population and more people had received the vaccines, many governments loosened such mandates considerably. By late 2022, masks were still encouraged but not required in most public settings, suggesting a degree of change due to the virus's continued impact and the effectiveness of vaccines. By mid-2023, most public places had eliminated masking requirements.

The shifts were seen in private entities too. Many hospitals and other health-related organizations imposed similar mask and vaccine mandates on their employees, with limited exceptions. These restrictions were loosened as the vaccine became more available as well. However, some entities continued to encourage the use of masks in certain settings through 2022, also suggesting change. Mask requirements had loosened considerably to be optional in various settings by mid-2023, and most COVID pandemic–related restrictions and policies had been lifted by 2024.

Managers at all levels of an organization and public officials must carefully plan how to phrase a message in order to get a desired response, especially as it pertains to challenging situations. Because each situation involves changing how people behave, these situations involve audience dynamics that must be accounted for in the message to get "buy-in" from the audience. Without that "buy-in," the effort is likely to fail or take longer to implement. However, management also needs to listen to people and pay attention to events within and outside the organization to understand potential risks and avert crises.

This text offers ways to formulate a message related to these most challenging communication situations. Leadership programming and guides commonly identify certain traits or attributes that impact successful leadership such as emotional intelligence, trustworthiness, motivation, and positivity. Many of these have some root in principles of rhetoric. This book is designed to help you make connections between these commonly understood leadership characteristics, neuroscience, and related elements of technical and professional communication embedded in the rhetoric of the message. Understanding the inter-related nature of these areas of thought will aid in crafting effective communication that addresses risk, crisis, and change.

A thread linking risk, crisis, and organizational change is that all of them involve the need to alter behavior in order to respond to the situation. If one is made aware of a potential risk of injury related to doing something, they have to pay closer attention when performing that activity to avoid experiencing that harm than they might otherwise. If faced with a crisis, one may need to change a routine, wearing a face mask to work, for example, when they usually did not. While it may be for a short period of time, it still affects behavior. A change to organizational strategy can force employees to have to change priorities, and a change in policy forces a change to everyone's behavior. So, change to varying degrees is involved with all of these situations.

Change makes many people nervous, because it represents a threat to a routine with which we are comfortable. Generally, surveys find that the most stressful events are those that involve change: death of a spouse, divorce, job loss. We are not sure how a change in behavior will impact us; we may be comfortable with the status quo simply because we know what to expect. We may not be able to anticipate how a change will impact us; consequently, there is some threat to our well-being—or our survival.

Understanding how an audience interprets a message about risks, crises, or changes is important to understanding how to shape the message for best effect. One's experiences in life affect their perception of reality and of situations, and the communicator needs to consider these effects. Scott noted that:

> [j]ust as the multidisciplinary field of risk communication has shifted from the transmittal of narrow, technical analyses and assessments of risk to psychological, social, and broader cultural considerations and models, approaches to [technical and professional communication] about risks have expanded to better account for sociocultural (including embodied, material, and political) contexts of risk meaning-making and experience.[2]

The most significant neuroscience-related connection between risk, crisis, and change is the impact each situation has on the basic instinct of survival; one's survival—life, well-being, or professional growth—is impacted to varying degrees with each situation. As the title of the book suggests, the sharing of narratives facilitates much of the change in behaviors associated with addressing risk, crisis, and change. However, sharing a story about one's or an organization's experience with a specific issue is not going to be effective unless it offers certain kinds of information that appeal to the audience. Further, risks, crises, and change associated with situations related to specialized technologies, medical/health sciences, or specialized practices require the application of certain tactics within those narratives. In this chapter, we explore some of those neuroscience and rhetoric elements with explicit links to those leadership traits. None is more important, though, than trust. An audience needs to trust the person in whose leadership they put their life or livelihoods (Flynn, 2015; Hoff-Clausen, 2013; Offerdal et al., 2021).[3–5] There are a number of ways to establish trustworthiness.

The Role of Trust

Necessarily, trustworthiness begins with the notion of establishing trust through communication habits and moves toward using that attribute to help employees and customers/clients respond with a good attitude. This extends to general public audiences as well. Scott noted that the study of risk communication was prompted, among other issues, from, "…the growing recognition of a disconnect between expert and public conceptions of risk, and a growing distrust in risk management authorities,…."[6] In a previous book, I described a compassionate approach to executive communication related to a variety of situations and settings.[7] Worth noting, is that I used the terms "trust" and "change" approximately 20 times in the first chapter of that book. So much of executive leadership revolves around the notion of change—whether imposed on an organization (as with the COVID-19 pandemic) or voluntarily sought (such as to address a decline in sales/relative economic downturn in the industry).

For example, the concept of trust in a speaker or source of information is directly related to the rhetorical principle of "ethos," or the source's credibility. Generally, if a tobacco farmer asserted that there was no relationship between cigarette smoking and cancer, most audiences would perceive bias; of course, the farmer does not want a negative health consequence associated with their crop, because it would negatively impact their income. However, if a physician were to make the same statement, an audience would likely perceive the statement as more credible. The physician has medical training and should have a better understanding of tobacco's health risks along with no vested interest in the tobacco industry; so, the physician would be considered a more credible source.

Another aspect of ethos is the audience's relationship with any media outlet from which it gets information. The propagation of social media and digital news sources brings with it potential for bias, even if unperceived by the audience. If a reader gets most of their information from a certain set of news media that it perceives to be unbiased, but actually has some degree of bias, that source is deemed credible by that audience. Until information presented by such sources is adequately proven to be false by the audience's standards, an audience will trust it. Such sources, also, are able to include images and video along with any text, in their pages. This brings various visual elements into consideration—demanding consideration of multimodal rhetoric.

Multiple Modes of Communication

Managers and executives communicate using many methods—email, phone, face-to-face, video conferencing, or document reporting. They, also, communicate through their actions. Actions convey messages visually and spatially, and a given audience may perceive them in various ways. Some of my previous books focused on principles of multimodal rhetoric and consideration of neuroscience elements in technical and professional communication, particularly in leadership positions.[8–11] I make reference to these throughout this book.

Also, a message is perceived by an audience relative to multiple interactions. An audience may witness a series of messages regarding related activities. What an executive/manager communicates in one setting can affect how another, somewhat related message is perceived in another setting.

Emotional Intelligence

"Emotional intelligence" is recognized as a common guiding principle related to leadership and management. Generally, the concept pertains to the use of an understanding of others' feelings and one's own feelings about a situation or issue in making decisions and communicating those decisions. Grabill and Simmons argued that risk communication should include input from the public relative to their experiences and participation in developing the message.[12] By engaging the public explicitly, a refined message emerges that shows consideration of the audience's perspective. If acted on appropriately, this understanding will enable the communicator to provide a message that the audience perceives as recognizing their concerns while helping them understand how they will benefit from acting on the message.

The Emotionally Intelligent Manager

Caruso and Salovey call attention to the importance of the role emotions have in decision-making and in response to decisions. Managers must understand how to use emotion—their own as well as those of others with whom they work—to craft an effective message on which an audience will respond favorably.

They describe the process by which to use this "intelligence" as:

1. Understand the situation, including the people involved.
2. Identify feelings of those involved.
3. Describe the focus of attention.
4. Understand emotions: why do people feel a certain way about the focus of attention.
5. Manage feelings of those involved.[13]

It may be necessary, due to economic conditions, to downsize regardless of employee performance. Through 2023 and 2024 we saw (and continue to see) organizations in a variety of fields—including scientific and technology-related fields—downsize because of economic pressures in the post-COVID world. In some cases, this downsizing included input from employees; in other cases, it did not include such input.

Emotional intelligence allows people to empathize with others, which facilitates the neuroscientific attribute associated with mirror neurons. Pillay notes that mirror neurons enable people to recognize shared experiences, affecting a perceived bond between them.[14] The effective manager mirrors the values of their employees as well as their superiors and models those values. When making decisions, one needs to mirror the decision-making process valued by those on that team.

Expanding on the concepts presented by Caruso and Salovey, Bradberry and Greaves (2009) provide some details and tips on relationship building (Chapter 8).

Relationship-building tips that involve communication explicitly include:

1. Enhance your own communication style, including the ability to adjust.
2. Avoid giving mixed signals.
3. Remember the little things that work.
4. Accept feedback graciously.
5. Build trust—including "consistency in words, action, behaviors over time" (p. 191).
6. Use anger purposefully.
7. Acknowledge others' emotions.
8. Explain decisions.[15]

As the adage states, "actions speak louder than words." People will quickly lose trust in us if our actions are contrary to our words. Our words and actions must mirror the values of the team(s) of which we are a member.

Further, items 7 and 8 recognize that, one should still exercise some degree of empathy or compassion even when communicating difficult decisions. Bradberry and Greaves explain that acknowledging others' feelings and explaining decisions that may upset people may mitigate negative attitudes toward change.[16]

Because many of the changes that companies or organizations have to communicate to the public is done by executives, some of these principles also apply to messages to those public audiences. The general public must feel a sense of trust in the speaker/communicator to be accepting of the change occurring.

The Neuroscience of Trust and Emotional Intelligence Within Narratives

Our memories of experiences with others mix with mirror neurons to process what we observe in others' actions and what we understand of them. These processes impact how we interpret the world. They help us reach conclusions about those observations of actions.

The more we see someone acting in a way that we value or in a way that reflects our values, the more favorably we will perceive the individual. If there is inconsistency between words and their actions, we may distrust the person. As I mentioned before, mirror neurons are active as one observes activity that one wants to emulate or with which one wants to assimilate.[17] Mirror neurons are involved in persuasion. An audience wants to mirror some aspect of the speaker, or the speaker may want to reflect some quality of the audience to assimilate with it more.

Mirror neurons help facilitate a shared experience between speaker and audience in persuasive contexts.[18] "Studies have found that trust is, perhaps, the most important attribute in persuasion."[19] Persuasion is the form of rhetoric most involved in communicating change, because an audience is likely to need to be persuaded to change.

This is important to the effectiveness of narratives in facilitating change, too. A narrative is a story about an experience that may be used to illustrate or develop a point. Narratives that illustrate how change in another setting came about successfully can help to encourage audiences to feel better about a similar change they may experience. Narratives also provide details about specific events that might suggest or demonstrate risk.

A narrative may be metaphorical in nature. Millar and Backer-Beck call attention to the phenomenon of metaphors of crisis.[20] They observe the concept of "war" as a common metaphor used to characterize responding to a crisis, including phrases like "War on drugs" to represent policies and plans to address the crisis drug abuse is taking on people.[21] Subsequently, they suggest using metaphors to characterize a risk or crisis. Such metaphors should provide a sort of generalized narrative to help an audience understand context and necessary action to address the situation. Metaphoric narratives are useful but limited. Specific stories tend to be more useful in persuading an audience to change behaviors or understand a situation.

Personal narratives, even third-person narratives (those describing someone else's experience) tend to be productive. They should come as close as possible to representing the situation an audience faces. If the narrative is positive, the hope is that their change mirrors the successful change of the narrative. Even if presented as an experience symptomatic of risk or danger, an audience will feel the narrator's experience because of mirror neurons. Further, such a story helps to build trust. Trust is part of persuasion; one cannot persuade someone of anything if the audience does not trust the speaker/writer. The closer a narrative comes to repeating or assimilating to an audience's experiences and perception of reality, the more the narrator is perceived as believable and trustworthy.

Another neuroscience concept associated with persuasion is "reward neurons." These neurons are activated when the audience perceives that certain action will be rewarded; they are motivated by that perceived reward to behave accordingly. If one is made aware of a particular reward associated with doing something, and they value that reward, they are more motivated to attain that reward. If the value of a given reward—one's safety, for example— is shared between the speaker and the audience, that value is mirrored; there may be an overlap between the impact of mirror neurons and reward neurons. If the narrative has a positive ending, the audience hopes to attain a similar outcome, which is perceived as a reward for changing behavior. If the narrative has a negative outcome that occurred due to a lack of changed behaviors or inadequate changes in behavior, though, the expectation for the speaker is that the audience will perceive the negative consequence of not changing behavior as a penalty or punishment.

Between these two kinds of neurons and the scholarship on emotional intelligence, there is a common thread; people like to know that they share common values and experiences with others they look up to or follow and are respected by these others. The identified principles of emotional intelligence focus on explicitly making connections with others' emotions—understanding their fears/concerns/values and balancing the needs of the task with their emotional needs.

Zak has noted connections between narrative, neuroscience, and trust. When an audience understands that they share a feeling or experience with the speaker, they come to trust the speaker because of the mirrored experiences and emotions.[22,23] Hagle asserts that hopeful, inspiring narratives can build trust due to the same mirroring dynamics. Hagle identifies four specific attributes of hopeful narratives:

1. They frame inspiring, long-term opportunity out in the future that can focus and motivate a large number of participants.
2. They identify trends that suggest the opportunity is in fact becoming more achievable.
3. They identify obstacles and challenges that stand in the way of achieving the opportunity.
4. They create an explicit call to action that will encourage people to come together and focus on increasing impact.[24]

The hopeful narrative serves as a basis for facilitating change in behaviors, whether it is to change direction generally, navigate through a crisis, or encourage caution to minimize risk. Applying an understanding of how mirror neurons and reward neurons operate helps advance this framework further.

The executive or official who is able to gain and maintain the trust of their employees or the public toward affecting changes in behavior can successfully balance the needs of the organization with the needs of their employees and the public. That trust extends to the public sphere when an organization's representative communicates the organization's plans for addressing risk, crisis, or change associated with its operations. Trust is intimately linked with neuroscience elements through narratives. Narratives also help to communicate with various audiences about technical topics by emphasizing relatable experiences rather than emphasizing technical terminology or concepts. We will see in later chapters how these ideas may be applied in specific settings, relating to risk, crisis, and change associated with technical communication.

Overview of Book

This book provides tools by which to use this combination through case study analyses and integration of scholarship, particularly narrative scholarship, across the phenomena of risk, crisis, and change management specific to technical situations. Narratives can take the form of experiences related to some kind of risk in an effort to helping others avoid and address risk. Experiences within crises help the organization and/or individual to navigate through crisis. Experiences of change help an organization and/or individual navigate through change. In each case, a narrative might inform about a yet to be perceived risk or crisis (descriptive narrative), it might be part of an internal dialogue about addressing a risk, crisis, or need to change as it happens (evaluative narrative), or it can reveal how other organizations or people addressed a similar situation, helping to address the current situation (prescriptive narrative). We will discuss all of these types and uses of narratives as we move through upcoming chapters.

Chapter 2 expands on the neuroscience concepts related to change that were introduced earlier in this chapter, and which are applied to information in other chapters. Indeed, multiple chapters pertain to elements related to change because of the nature of risk, crisis, and change generally. Communication of accidents or incidents in technical settings is discussed to establish basic elements of using narratives to affect change in behavior. Each situation—risk, crisis, and change, is, then, treated more specifically. First, concepts and examples of rhetorical analyses describe the application of specific topics and tips. Then, we will engage in case analysis activities to reflect as to how lessons learned in the case might apply to a similar situation and consider how the addressing of risk, crisis, or change in the case might apply more broadly. Because each case is based on a relatively recent situation, more information may be found online that sheds further light on how the case evolved or ended.

CHAPTER 2

How Narratives Influence Trust

Cognition and Persuasion

As we saw in Chapter 1, persuasion is key to addressing all three of the situations covered in this book—risk, crisis, and change. In this chapter, we examine detail-specific connections between principles of multimodal persuasive rhetoric and neuroscience that are broken down further in subsequent sections of the book. At the most basic level, rhetoric of any type must consider the audience's perception of the world, which is affected by cognition; and cognition is affected by neurobiological phenomena.

Cognition is generally defined to include perception and understanding of the world as well as learning and comprehension. Persuasion involves one's perception of a given situation; that is, how does one perceive a crisis, for example? A crisis generally invokes some degree of anxiety in most people; however, one's previous experiences with different kinds of crises will likely affect how they respond to a given situation that may be deemed a crisis. If a person, for example, has experience with several crises that are similar to the one that is about to occur, they will likely respond less anxiously than one who has never experienced such crises.

I have noted before that, "Aristotle made the connection between rhetoric and biology (Aristotle, transl. 1991)."[1,2] A growing body of scholarship in cognitive neuroscience is helping leaders understand why certain messages and how they are presented affect an audience. This is why it is important to consider neuroscientific attributes that are involved in multimodal persuasive messages.

The multitude of digital news sources and social media contribute much to dynamics involved in how audiences perceive situations. Simons and Jones encourage integrating the full range of resources and tools humans have to communicate.[3]

Intersecting Theories

In this chapter, we will consider a brief summary of theories linking multimodal persuasive rhetoric and neuroscience to risk, crisis, and change communication. Scholarship from several different fields is synthesized in this book to maximize connections across them relative to this communication. Just within the field of neuroscience, scholarship is "spread across multiple disciplines."[4] These include cognitive neuroscience, biological neuroscience, and cognitive psychology. Further, scholarship from different technical fields is integrated in the book, drawing upon research, practices, and discourse of experts and practitioners in those technical fields.

Meaning is a social construct; one's interpretation of images and events evolves through interactions with others. Cognition is rhetorical and social. It takes interaction with the world around us to comprehend a situation and the meaning of the information provided. Our own experiences and the narratives that we share with others and that others share with us shape our understanding of the world. Cognitive science, generally, recognizes these attributes of cognition—social and biological attributes related to facilitating an understanding of our world. However, the discussion of these cognitive neuroscience dynamics is complicated by disciplinary discourses and exclusions.

Aristotle[5] and Perelman and Olbrechts-Tyteca[6] recognized that one must adjust their message to account for attributes of a particular audience. Such acknowledgment requires including physiological attributes in the cognitive equation. If the audience's cognitive capacities and understanding of the world are not considered in developing the message, the message's meaning is lost. As Perelman and Olbrechts-Tyteca acknowledge, the most important rule of rhetoric is to adapt the message to the audience.[7] A message is not automatically understood just because it is articulated; it must be conveyed in a way that suits the audience's background and understandings, their experiences and practices, and their capacity for cognition.

Persuasive Rhetoric

As stated above, Perelman and Olbrechts-Tyteca[8] provide a foundation for linking persuasive rhetoric and neuroscience. However, some other principles of persuasive rhetoric need to be considered as well. Persuasion includes the assumption that the audience is willing to change their perception of a given situation such that a reasonably persuasive message could affect that change. For example, one may not care how a virus might impact them personally until a friend or colleague is affected by that virus. Consequently, any communication they receive about the potential risks of that virus are not heeded until the friend or colleague tells them about how it affected them. Relating to the COVID-pandemic period, in spite of appeals by public health and government officials, many people refused to get vaccinated or wear a mask. They were not willing to change their position that they should not have to get vaccinated or wear a mask.

Another basic component of persuasion is the various ways an audience may be moved to change its perception: logos (reason/logic), ethos (speaker's/writer's credibility), and pathos (appeal to emotion). A combination of approaches works best. If a relatively healthy friend of yours caught COVID-19, for example, and you saw him or her experience considerable suffering from it for several weeks, that experience may be enough to encourage you to take precautions to avoid getting it—such as using a mask regularly. That experience combines elements of ethos (your close friend—a credible source) and logos (you observed their experience firsthand and understand its reality).

Perelman and Olbrechts-Tyteca[9] argued that perception is subjective rather than objective, further developing the point that one's understanding of the world is affected by experiences rather than a uniform logic. The subjective nature of perception complicates communication to large audiences, especially those that may have varying viewpoints and backgrounds. Always, whether communicating internally or externally, the executive has to consider how to present a message that meets the needs of multiple audiences. If there is a value or variable that is common across different audiences, that may be used as a focus by which to frame the message.

Using the COVID case example above, you may have several friends, many of whom are not aware that your friend, Robert, had COVID and suffered for several weeks. You share the story of Robert's experience with your other friends, even including a detailed description of the coughing fits that he had. He was in relatively good general health when he caught it, too; yet, he suffered for quite some time before recovering. He may even have developed "long COVID"—a term generally applied to characterize ongoing health effects from the COVID virus such as shortness of breath or memory lapses among other symptoms. Those other friends hear or read of Robert's experience and may even follow up by speaking with him (direct communication with trusted source) and/or reading articles from credible sources about those symptoms. Because the sources of information are valued commonly among the larger group of friends, they all become more concerned about ways they could avoid being exposed to COVID.

Multimodal Rhetoric

As indicated above, various modes of representation affect an audience's ability to make meaning about the information provided with those combinations. The New London Group[10] was among the first to identify how combinations of modes of representation can affect audience cognition, perception, and meaning-making. They list particular modes: verbal (words), visual (images), aural (sound), spatial, and touch. Multimodal rhetoric would include any combination of these; for example, a video may combine visual and aural modes of representation. A speech might include aural, visual, and spatial modes as the speaker moves about a room and shows visual aids as they speak.

Sheridan, Ridolfo, and Michel noted that, "[h]umans experience the world through multiple senses simultaneously... A speech delivered in a public forum is a complex performance that involves not just words, but gestures, facial expressions, intonation and more..."[11] These different forms of representation—aural, visual, spatial—facilitate cognition.

While the field of rhetoric has treated multimodality as means of facilitating meaning-making and cognition, neuroscience has also found value in the concept of multimodality. Neurons respond to stimuli, and the various modes of representation act as different kinds of stimuli. Neuroscience scholarship has found that some neurons are multimodal. This link is natural and logical for two other reasons.

Multimodality of Neurons

Neurobiological scholarship identifies two types of neurons relative to modal attributes: unimodal and multimodal. While unimodal neurons can carry stimuli from a single mode—auditory, for example, multimodal neurons can carry information relative to more than one mode—from both visual and auditory senses, for example.[12] Further, studies suggest optimal combinations of modes to facilitate better cognition than others.[13-15] We will consider some critique of these combinations within cases presented in later chapters.

Social Media and Perceived Response

An emerging phenomenon with respect to audience reaction to risk, crisis, and change communication efforts is how certain actions are represented and perceived. So, no longer is it just the risk or crisis that moves people to action, but the way the stated response action is represented (outrageous versus reasonable) and their response—agreement/disagreement—with the representation impacts whether they will take the necessary action conveyed. This was seen between 2020 and 2024 not only in the debate regarding masking and vaccines but within debates about Critical Race Theory as well as abortion. Malecki et al. found, relative to the specific dynamics with COVID-19, that, "In concert, hazard and outrage along with cultural and economic context shape adherence to, and overall acceptance of, personal mitigation strategies including wearing facemasks and social distancing among the general public."[16]

This complicates how a message may be presented; if an audience with conservative views respects a speaker who is perceived as trustworthy and who recommends certain action to address a crisis the audience will likely perceive the message as reasonable. For example, President Donald Trump, who was President of the United States as COVID-19 emerged as a pandemic crisis, is known to have received a vaccination for COVID during his presidency; however, he never issued a vaccine mandate. Conservative audiences generally believed that masking and getting vaccinated should be personal choices and not mandated.

Again, considering Robert's COVID case as sharing of narratives about it, the more members of Robert's social circle see and hear about his case—perhaps even seeing images on one of his social media accounts of him in a hospital bed—the more impact the general message has about the risks of getting it. The audience knows and respects "Robert"; they hear or read about his experience in a narrative; and they see the effects of the COVID experience with the images of him in a hospital bed—perhaps using a ventilator. The images become a visual element of the narrative. If there is a video of him in the midst of a coughing fit, that becomes another part of the narrative, and the audience perceives real risks.

How an audience perceives the communicator affects their perception of the message itself. In rhetoric scholarship, this is called "ethos," or the speaker's credibility. In other words, an audience will consider how trustworthy the speaker conveying the message is. The more trustworthy the audience perceives the communicator, the more the message itself will be valued. Neuroscience concepts outlined in this chapter are involved in the biology of trust. Understanding those concepts will enable the reader to better understand the effect certain communication about change has on an audience.

A Framework for Understanding the Neuroscience of Trust in Communication About Technical or Scientific Topics

People rely on their memory and what they have learned to help them understand how to deal with situations. Memory is based on education, training, experience, and learning. Memory that is based on experiences can come from multiple sources—me, someone close to me—a friend or relative, or someone with whom I am unfamiliar but may be an expert. With technical or scientific topics, one needs to place trust in the expertise of another with whom they may unfamiliar. A basic element of technical communication is to adjust to the audience's level of understanding of a topic or concept. In some cases, this means using lay terminology rather than specialized terminology. This may, also, involve relating to the audience using metaphors the recipients will understand. However, narratives of experiences with the specific technical or scientific topic may help the audience better understand how to change their behavior to address related risks, crises, or needed changes.

As a narrative is shared, experience is shared, and one relates the experience to the new situation. The narrative provides information: what did I/they do; was the outcome good/bad (reward neurons); what would I/they do differently? A person who may not be an expert in a technical field can share their own experience about an event related to that field with someone else who is not an expert. That information can help the audience member understand how they could respond to a similar situation, even without knowing much about the technical dynamics at work.

A key element affecting one's perception of the narrative and "lessons" from it is the degree to which one trusts the source. Of course, one trusts their own credibility. However, to what degree does one trust someone else's credibility, especially with respect to technical matters about which one may understand less? The more someone mirrors my values or experiences while understanding my relationship to the specialized subject, the more I would trust them (mirror neurons). If I do not know who the person is other than their educational background, I may perceive one as a relevant expert and trust their insight. However, I need to know that they appreciate my experience with the topic and can relate to that experience.

A graphic represents these dynamics of trust affecting response to persuasive rhetoric emerges (Figure 2.1).

As noted in Figure 2.1, trust is impacted by several elements related to neuroscience, specifically concepts of mirroring and rewarding. Because narratives represent the sharing of experiences or prescribing behaviors, the relationship between trust and perception of mirroring and rewards

Source of Change decision	Source of information related to change/ transition	Level of trust in Source	Level of mirroring to me
Self	Self/close friend	High	Exact
Other	Friend/acquaintance to stranger	Low to high (depends on perception of expertise valued relative to trustworthiness)	Not at all to very close

Figure 2.1 Relationship between Trust and response to persuasive rhetoric

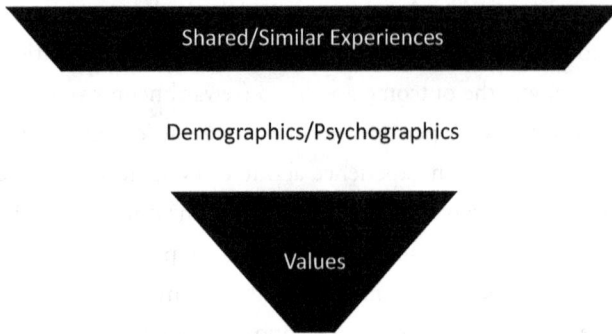

Figure 2.2 Factors affecting trust relative to mirroring

needs to be considered. Figure 2.2, further, suggests a breakdown of factors affecting trust specifically relative to mirroring others.

The closer that the relevant expert can mirror me, the more trustworthy I will find them; the more I will feel connection to them.

Ways to Mirror Me (The More That Apply, The Better):

Each of the following three categories represents ways others might mirror us or that we might mirror others. However, taken separately, they represent certain degrees of mirroring.

Shared Values

No matter how educated, experienced, or enculturated a set of people are, if they share a common belief system and common understanding of systems, they feel a connection to each other. For example, if you attend a religious service, those attending likely have a certain belief system common to them—a set of values. There may be some variation relative to certain details, but generally, they hold to a certain set of beliefs of right and wrong/good and bad.

Demographics/Psychographics

People of similar ethnicity and economic background tend to feel a bond with each other that goes beyond basic values. Even if some differences exist in values—one is a Christian while another is Jewish—they understand a common bond through being white, or because they both have a graduate degree in business or a science field. Further, they may live in similar communities.

Shared Experiences

Do you tend to vacation in the same place each year at about the same time? Do you have friends/acquaintances who have vacationed there, too? Did you talk with them about their vacation and compare it to yours? Did you attend a community event and know someone you saw there with whom you stopped and talked? Did you attend the same event and find out later that someone else you knew attended it? Did you ask them about it or compare your experience at the event with theirs? Did you experience anything about which you could relate a story after someone had just mentioned that they had experienced something similar to what you had?

These situations represent shared or similar experiences to which people can relate to each other. The more closely our experiences seem similar to those of others, the closer we feel to them; their experiences have mirrored ours. The details of these may overlap so much as to suggest a deeper mirroring to us than even similar educational background.

As we just considered, the more of these shared elements that overlap with ours, the closer we will feel to other people. If an engineer had vacationed on Hilton Head Island in the vicinity where a local bank employee vacationed and the two happen upon each other at a community event, each wearing a Hilton Head Island t-shirt, they may stop and talk about Hilton Head Island and their experiences there. They may even develop a friendship, having also shared attendance at the community event, suggesting they may live in the same community.

While a mirror displays visual elements, our mirror needs to reflect shared experiences and values, which are conveyed through narratives. Whether it is someone in a position of leadership communicating a decision about risk, crisis, or change or an employee identifying a potential risk or crisis, the description of the decision-making process or details shared in the description shape how the message is received and per-ceived. The closer the message mirrors the audience's values, the better it may be understood and received.

Two other considerations that affect one's attitude and ability to change behavior are the degree of change one must make and the con-sequences of not changing. The greater the change, the more one needs to trust that good will come of it and the change will not be as challeng-ing as it may seem. So, a minor change to behavior related to avoiding risk will not take much trust to act upon. However, a long-term change in job responsibilities due to budget cuts—especially if taking on more responsibilities is involved—will require faith that supervisors will not be overly critical during the adjustment period while assuring continued employment.

These responses to change may be associated with reward neurons; what benefit that I value will come if I/the organization make(s) the stated change? Alternatively, or in conjunction (depending on the situation), what negative consequence of significance may result if I/the organization do(es) not change?

Bringing these components together, a framework for understanding links between narratives, neuroscience, and motivating change behavior emerges.

I: Degree of Trust in Information Source
II: Degree of Stated Change Needed (time frame/behavior)
   A: Short term/Long term
   B: Behavior change
III: Consequences—good/bad relative to personal and/or organiza-tional values.
   A: Positive
   B: Negative

Finally, synthesizing many of the elements identified so far, a rubric is presented that can be used to measure the effectiveness of a narrative to motivate change (Figure 2.3).

In Chapter 3, we will consider the relationship between narratives and motivation to changing behaviors, identifying several studies that

Attribute	Highly effective	Effective	Less effective	Ineffective
Trust in Source	High: felt connection	Moderately High: Shared values	Moderate: shared values but some personal disconnect	Low
Time Frame for Change Behavior	Reasonable; easy transition period	Reasonable; faster-paced period	Fast; not much time to adjust	Too fast
Consequences: Positive	Clearly stated and real	Clearly stated and real; less common outcome	Less clearly stated/based on metaphor	Vague/entirely based on metaphor; or outcome very unique (unlikely to occur)
Consequences: Negative	Clearly stated and real	Clearly stated and real; less common outcome	Less clearly stated/based on metaphor	Vague/entirely based on metaphor; or outcome very unique (unlikely to occur)

Figure 2.3 Persuasion–Trust rubric

provide evidence of the effectiveness of narratives to motivate change in behaviors. These contribute to a more advanced rubric for assessing the effectiveness of narratives related to risk, crisis, and change in technical communication contexts.

CHAPTER 3

Narratives That Influence Change

As we noted in the two previous chapters, narratives—the sharing of details of specific experiences—are valuable vehicles for communicating messages that affect one's perception of security and safety. For instance, we share stories about our experiences after we have been involved in an accident or something strange happened to us. These stories not only inform our audience of a risk we faced but they connect the experience to their own experiences. Narratives are useful for helping to detect or anticipate risk, and they are valuable in communicating specific risk and how to address risks, manage crises, and adapt to change. A framework for considering how the variables associated with changing behaviors was presented in Chapter 2. This chapter provides more detail into how narratives work within technically oriented messages and their effectiveness in changing behaviors.

Narratives Change Behaviors

When reporting accidents, we often want to understand specific details of the event. A police report of an auto accident includes such detail. The more detail that is included, the better an audience can understand the situation, what may have caused the accident, and how people responded to the situation. In the next chapter, more information is shared about how narratives are used in various technical fields to identify potential risks and facilitate change. Flynn also acknowledges that the information shared in a narrative becomes part of new knowledge for an audience, and "[t]o resolve the cognitive dissonance, individuals begin to change their attitude to one that is more consistent with the new information in their mental framework."[1]

Dahlstrom encourages using analogous narratives to help people in nontechnical fields understand the need for change and how it can be successful. He states, "[r]esearch suggests that narratives are easier to comprehend and audiences find them more engaging than traditional logical-scientific communication…. narratives can also present themselves within larger messages as testimonials, exemplars, case studies, or eyewitness accounts."[2] Again, a basic principle of technical communication is adjusting to the audience's education level and familiarity with a specific technical or scientific topic. People respond well to specific cases/anecdotes that illustrate successful changes and details of how change occurred. Providing such details when communicating change can limit resistance and create a positive attitude.

Likewise, a narrative that is included as part of instructional information helps to relate the information to the audience, potentially motivating them to change their behavior. This is where some elements of multimodal communication come into play. A number of experimental studies have ascertained a link between exposure to narratives and motivation to change behaviors in health- and safety-related contexts. Several scholarly articles on the subject have been published since the early 2000s, many since 2015.

Several experimental studies connected to the use of narratives in providing information about certain conditions within healthcare find explicit and statistically significant links between narrative and influence on behavior. In each study, the information shared with participants includes technical concepts phrased with the audience's background in mind, applying a basic element of technical communication—adjusting to the audience. For at least one of the study groups involved, the researcher adds a narrative or series of narratives to information and studies responses related to intent to change behavior or directly observes related behavior.

Marty and McDermott[3,4] found that male college student participants who listened to a narrative of a patient's experience with testicular cancer motivated them to seek screening and conduct self-examination more often than did a similar group that only received a printed pamphlet with only factual information. Rook[5] found that female participants who read a case history about a woman with osteoporosis motivated participants to change eating habits more so than did participants who read an abstract message about the condition. Larkey and Gonzalez[6] found that Latino participants who listened to a story of a colorectal cancer patient conveyed intention to change their diet more so than did Latino participants who read straight factual information about colorectal cancer. Kim et al.[7] also found that the inclusion of narratives in news that described examples about successful cessation of smoking had a greater influence on motivating intention to quit smoking than did news stories that excluded such narratives.

Interestingly, Cox and Cox[8] found that female participants who read material promoting mammograms and that included a narrative about a woman with breast cancer that had a negative outcome (woman died from it after not seeking early detection) were more motivated to seek early detection for breast cancer than were participants who read similar information that included a narrative with a positive outcome (woman who was saved because she sought early detection). A similar finding comes from Hillenbrand and Verrina,[9] who reported that narratives related to economic decisions impacted perception of social behaviors and motivation to act toward the social good (rather than selfishly). In their study, they found that negative narratives (reporting selfish behavior rather than prosocial behavior) were deemed to be even more effective in encouraging prosocial behaviors than were positive narratives. Such findings suggest that, depending on the situation, narratives that relate a negative outcome caused by not changing behavior may work in conjunction with narratives showing positive outcomes toward motivating intent to change behavior. The audience sees both the benefit of changing behavior as well as the drawback of not changing behavior.

One may consider the ad campaign "Tips from Former Smokers" as evidence of this impact. The ads, developed by the Centers for Disease Control and Prevention, feature real people who smoked for a period of time and who talk about experiences dealing with cancers related to their smoking. Many of these ads show graphic images of people wearing medical equipment or having had their physical appearance altered by related surgeries. In some, a post-testimonial message is shown acknowledging when the person died after making the advertisement. Murphy-Hoefer et al.[10] conducted a study on the effectiveness of the campaign, which covered the years 2012 to 2018. They reported that the campaign motivated over 16 million people to attempt to quit smoking, while over one million were able to sustain smokeless habits.

Some studies related to construction safety have found similar outcomes. Ricketts[11] found that the integration of narratives within safety instructions for building a swing set improved compliance with related behaviors and immediate recall of safety tips than did instructions that did not include narratives. These studies indicate that narratives affect behaviors to address risks.

Multimodal Narrative

The various modes of delivery included in the range of studies identified above are important, too. Note that some featured only print-linguistic documentation, some of which included visual graphics, while others integrate audio and/or video. The measured impact of the combination of image and audio narrative in the anti-smoking campaign shows the effectiveness of using such combinations. These images included former smokers who are now disfigured or have limited abilities due to their smoking and cancer-related treatments.

Narrative and Change Neuroscience

Jeff Bezos, CEO of Amazon, begins each executive meeting with members reviewing a narrative text, leading to discussion.[12] Denning[13] and Saltmarshe identify several ways narrative works to help people understand and accept change. According to Saltmarsh,[14]

> Story has many different qualities that make it useful for the work of systems change. It's a direct route to our emotions, and therefore important to decision-making. It creates meaning out of patterns. It coheres communities. It engenders empathy across difference. It enables the possible to feel probable in ways our rational minds can't comprehend. When it comes to changing the values, mindsets, rules, and goals of a system, story is foundational.

The author goes on to indicate that story helps to establish community and empathy—engaging emotional intelligence. "This work can make the possible feel more probable, bring new perspectives that challenge the goals and mindsets of a system, and enable the transformation of rules and processes." Indeed, Zak[15] identifies the effect narrative has on the body's own oxytocin as the reason for its effectiveness. Oxytocin moderates feelings of social bonding that affect mirror neurons as well as reward neurons.

There has been some study about the effectiveness of fictional narratives; that is, narratives that are not real cases but integrate elements that could be real. However, findings related to these situations are mixed. Flynn[16] notes that studies have found that viewers who watched a documentary on mental illness changed their perception of mental illness more readily than those who watched a fictional show about it, even though both shows covered the same issues. The more real the story is, the more it affects perception of reality and makes the prospects of change feel less threatening. Flynn identifies several attributes that impact one's response to attempts to change attitudes; these include, but are not limited to, counterarguing, avoidance, perceived norms and biases, self-efficacy, and expected outcomes. Generally, the more an audience trusts the narrator, the more effective the narrative is, and there are ways the narrator can facilitate trust.

The more time people have to develop counterarguments, which may come in the form of a counternarrative, the more they can resist change and reinforce their own position. The deeper a narrative can appeal to an audience, the less they have time to think of counterarguments. A story should not be so long as to lose one's attention, but it should be engaging enough that the audience thinks it through and can apply it to their own life. The more the audience trusts the speaker, the easier it is for them to change their behavior accordingly, too.

Avoidance is the desire not to deal with negative news. The longer one can avoid having to act on something, the less it affects them. So, the change narrative needs to convey a point when the change will begin and encourage people to act on it.

People will act in alliance with perceived norms; if the change can be presented as "normal" within the business or economic/organizational cycle, it is less threatening. A narrative can describe historical changes the organization went through at other times, showing it has lasted through similar situations.

Trust goes a long way toward addressing any perceived biases. This is an important reason why having employees' trust helps them accept change much faster than if they do not trust the organization/management. Management is often perceived as biased toward upper management, not caring much about lower management and its employees.

Part of what scares people about change is that they do not know if they can do it—self-efficacy toward change. Can they manage it? How does it affect them? What will things look like for them once it occurs? Acknowledging these common questions and exercising emotional intelligence will help management build appropriate outcome statements into messages. The goal is to help employees understand what they, not just the organization, will look like.

Narratives Help to Accept Change

A final issue that affects success in change is the time it takes to implement it. Heidari-Robinson and Heywood, noted that "[r]esearchers at the University of Michigan have also found that persistent job insecurity—for example, when a reorg takes much longer than it is supposed to—has a greater effect on health among workers than actual unemployment."[17] Once change is announced, regular communication is needed to let people know how it is proceeding and when certain benchmarks will be attained. Further, people need reassurance that they still have a job; or, if their position is likely to be terminated, they need time to transition to another position and reassurance that the organization will help with that.

These issues involved with change acceptance link directly to Flynn's points about avoidance and expected outcomes. If the organization is taking too long to change, it offers the employee a reason to avoid dealing with change issues and modifies their beliefs about expected outcome—"maybe the change won't happen at all."

Few people enjoy being surprised when they are not at Disney World or are the guest of honor at a surprise birthday party. Most people need to be eased into the idea of change. The first message employees at any level of the organization receive about the forthcoming change should NOT be "We need to change, and this is how we will do it." Instead, spend a few meetings letting employees and other audiences know about the potential for upcoming change, what it may involve and toward what ends/objectives it would be implemented.

"We are likely facing some changes to the way we market [X], and we are looking into what it would entail," allows the audience to absorb the idea of upcoming change without immediate action. They have a chance to think through several emotions.

Two days later: "We're getting a better idea of what's going on with the changes I mentioned a few days ago. We need more information about x, y, and z, though. We'll be inviting input from A, B and C."

This message allows them to understand progress is being made, and they may have a chance to provide some input. They will begin thinking about that input toward being productive with the change. This also allows those who want to have a say in the change or how it is implemented have that agency. This input may come in the form of narratives or short answers about concerns or experiences. Allowing employees and middle/lower management to participate in change planning can alleviate some angst.

In addition to the attention-getting messages prefacing change, the preparation messages and implementation messages should include narratives that help all connect positive experiences of change to what the organization will experience.

The studies summarized in this chapter help to further refine the rubric offered in Chapter 2 toward understanding of how narratives can be effective in communicating about risk, crises, and change in technical communication contexts (Figure 3.1).

Management Narratives

Management narratives will focus on stories of organizational changes. They can combine stories of successful change with stories of unsuccessful change, emphasizing how the organization's change will emulate that of successful changes. They can focus entirely on stories describing successful change. If employees trust management, they will likely believe these narratives, feeling better about the upcoming change. How much management shows it cares about employees and facilitating any changes they will experience professionally will also impact how willing employees are to be part of the needed change.

Attribute	Highly effective	Effective	Less effective	Ineffective
Trust in Source	High: felt connection	Moderately High: shared values	Moderate: shared values but some personal disconnect	Low
Technical Terminology Used	None used	Limited; characterized in simple terms	Limited: analogy provided	More terms used but not characterized
Explicitness of Change Stated	Clear, detailed	Clear, less detailed	Less clear	Vague
Degree of Change Stated	Seems reasonable/not dramatic	Reasonable/ a bit dramatic	Reasonable/ more dramatic	Too much/very dramatic
Time Frame for Change Behavior	Reasonable; easy transition period	Reasonable; faster-paced period	Fast; not much time to adjust	Too fast
Multimodal Delivery of Message	Print, audio, and visual	Audio and video	Print and image	Print only
Image Type, If Included	Real person(s)/same organization	Real person(s)/ not same organization	AI-generated	Drawn or clip art
Consequences: Positive	Clearly stated and real	Clearly stated and real; less common outcome	Less clearly stated/based on metaphor	Vague/entirely based on metaphor; or outcome very unique (unlikely to occur)
Consequences: Negative	Clearly stated and real	Clearly stated and real; less common outcome	Less clearly stated/based on metaphor	Vague/entirely based on metaphor; or outcome very unique (unlikely to occur)

Figure 3.1 Narrative-change effectiveness rubric

Employee Narratives

Employee narratives focus on specific individuals within an organization—how the change affected them personally and/or professionally. These are the stories that will have a more immediate impact on employees; so, they need to be genuine, relatable, and emphasize the consideration given to the transitioning employee from management.

Even if employees had to be let go, if their story can be positive—characterizing how the organization helped them find new employment and provided mental health assistance with that transition—employees generally will feel positive about the change. In online posts about loss of employment as a result of organizational change, former employees frequently decry the organization's lack of help with finding new employment and the feeling of being treated merely as a number by the organization's management. Testimonies about the consideration specific people personally received from the organization as they were let go is powerful—whether positive or negative.

Public Narratives

External audience narratives also have a powerful impact on organizational perception and reputation. First-hand stories from members of the public affected by organizational changes and narratives about how an organization responded to risk or crises carry considerable weight with existing and potential customers/clients and the public in general. External stakeholders are likely to respond more favorably when they trust the source of the change narrative and the narrative somehow relates to them, showing concern for their well-being and describing how they can benefit in the situation.

Subsequent chapters in this book provide more details about the application of narratives in various situations. Specific cases are included in the chapters to illustrate application of these concepts while providing activities to facilitate further thought and discussion. With each case, the framework provided in Chapter 2 and the rubric in this chapter will help to facilitate analyses, and the discussion questions will provide opportunities for application of the concepts. Chapter 4 presents specific cases related to risk, the least severe of changes among the set considered within this book. A crisis situation that led to changes in policy and practices toward reducing certain risks is also provided.

CHAPTER 4

Incident and Accident Reports in Technical Settings: Short Stories About Risk That Contributes to Change

Many technical fields include very dangerous situations in which incidents or accidents may occur. Incidents can be defined as any safety or health event that involves unintended results. Accidents are characterized as unintended events that result in some injury to a person or damage to property. Accidents or incidents may be related to specific problems with machinery/equipment (e.g.: engineering) some combination of equipment and human error (e.g.: construction), environmental factors affecting physical dynamics associated with an activity (e.g.: flight), medical emergencies (e.g.: nursing/healthcare), and others. Because of the potential for such occurrences, most technical fields have some kind of accident/incident reporting system, which may be internal to the organization or required at the state and/or federal level.

In addition to recording and documenting the incident/accident, the purpose of these reports is to identify risks toward making potential changes to improve safety and reduce those risks. Most of the time, the initial report is a completed templated form of varying length. While many of these forms use mostly templated items that involve short responses or checking off boxes, many also include space to include a narrative or description of the event that occurred. Additionally, many of these narratives and forms include an opportunity for the writer to provide recommend changes.

A description excerpted from a sample hospital incident report follows:

...a medication error incident occurred at [hospital and location identified]....

The error was identified by Nurse Jane Smith during a routine check of patient medication records against administered dosages. Upon discovering the discrepancy, Nurse Smith immediately informed the attending physician, Dr. Lisa Ray, and the hospital's pharmacy department...

In response to this incident, the following corrective actions have been implemented:[1]

Studies have found that these narratives help clarify potential risks and recommend ways to address them better than mere box-checking. Ray et al.[2] found that such narratives helped to identify 3.4 times more risk attributes than tabulated data alone in construction accident reporting, and they found that narratives identified almost 92 percent of risks not reported in tabled data. Further, a 2012 report published by the Department of Health and Human Services found that hospitals generally have an internal reporting system for cases of patient harm to Medicare beneficiaries; and while most of these are not effective for reporting such cases, 70 percent of the incidents that nurses reported related to Medicare recipients resulted in investigations, and 12.5 percent resulted in policy changes.[3]

Safety engineers rely on narratives within reports of accidents/incidents to generate precautions. Menon and Rainer link attributes of such narratives to public understanding of risks and ways for engineers to improve safety:

We acknowledge that seasoned engineers are unlikely to rely on the story of an engineering problem to provide them with their full understanding of it. However, safety-critical engineering is a discipline which relies on communication and public understanding of risk. ...and adequate communication—including in the form of accessible stories—is a necessary first step towards that.[4]

The authors' list of characteristics for successful safety engineering stories includes:

- The story must be an accurate model of the engineering problem.
- The story and any engineering solution to the problem should not be mixed in the presentation.
- Metaphors and assumptions within the story should be well-understood and, so far as possible, parallel the details of the engineering problem.
- The story must contain an element of drama, such as the potential for a fatal outcome for one or more characters.[5]

Airline passengers often share experiences in online forums or directly with air carriers. Peregrine acknowledges that "a study conducted by the Aviation Safety Network highlighted that airlines utilizing passenger feedback mechanisms observed a 20 percent reduction in safety incidents within a year. This demonstrates that timely information is crucial for immediate adjustments to protocols." She lists three specific areas that such reports can benefit from:

- Identifying weaknesses in training programs.
- Assessing the effectiveness of existing safety measures.
- Understanding passenger perceptions of risk.[6]

The airline industry has several reporting tools related to incidents or accidents that may occur. Various forms provide templated items to include in such reporting. Most of these are either short responses or checking a box. However, a few include sections that facilitate a detailed description of the event. A few examples of the narrative section are shown in Figures 4.1 and 4.2:

NARRATIVE HISTORY OF FLIGHT (Please type or print in ink.)

Describe what occurred in chronological order, including circumstances leading to and
nature of accident/incident. Describe terrain and include wreckage distribution sketch
if pertinent. Attach extra sheets if needed. State departure time and location, services
obtained, and intended destination. Provide as much detail as possible.

OPERATOR/OWNER SAFETY RECOMMENDATION (How could this accident/
incident have been prevented?)

From: NTSB 6120.1 Pilot/Operator Aircraft Accident/Incident Report. Courtesy: National
Transportation Safety Board

Figure 4.1 Narrative portion from Form NTSB 6120

Each example includes substantial space for a written description of
the event/incident. The first invites the writer to include a sketch (visual
representation) of the wreckage.

Note the space in the first example for providing a recommendation.
The National Business Aviation Association maintains examples of these
narratives as instructional tools for pilots. An example from that site
shows a recommendation that introduces changes to how training occurs:

> After thoroughly discussing the sequence of events, he asked for
> a written report—since he was not privy to the original ASAP

SUMMARY
J1. Summary—Provide a brief summary for all the MORs in this section that will provide enough information for QA to understand what occurred. Include information about items that require additional information in the specific MOR you are reporting.

Courtesy: National Transportation Safety Board

Figure 4.2 Narrative portion from Form NTSB 7210

report—and my suggestions to prevent a recurrence. I recommended the following:

- Thoroughly brief the incident to our pilots at our next quarterly pilot meeting. Since we routinely operate through this airport and FBO, the distraction and familiarity I fell prey to could happen to any one of us.
- Change our SOPs to explicitly disallow any other duties/ activities by either pilot as a runway is approached until either the aircraft is stopped short (hold short clearance) or completely across (cleared across clearance).
- Consider designating this runway/taxiway intersection as a "Hotspot" on the taxi diagram. The narrative should state that the visual volume of activity on the FBO ramp can cause distraction as the runway is approached.

...The ASAP program directly increased the level of safety at this airport (at least in our department) and avoided a violation on my otherwise clear, 41-year flying record.[7]

Of particular note with this narrative is the use of specialized acronyms (e.g.; FBO) and terminology (e.g.: "stopped short [hold short clearance]"). The general public would not understand these terms; however, the targeted audience would understand them. So, a lesson is that the use of specialized terms within a narrative is acceptable when the audience will understand them.

Another example of the narrative portion of a flight incident report shows some details included:

> The pilot of the tail wheeled-equipped airplane reported that he was on approach to land at an uncontrolled airport behind two helicopters. An airport surveillance video showed the accident airplane flying over the runway about 20 seconds after a helicopter was in slow hover taxi adjacent to the runway. The pilot reported that he saw the helicopter and decided to land long to maintain separation. He added that while on short final he saw a helicopter "cross" the runway, so he increased engine power to full and attempted a go-around. About one-third of the way down the length of the runway the airplane encountered the helicopter's downwash, and the airplane entered an uncommanded steep right bank. The pilot applied opposite aileron, but he was not able to maintain control of the airplane. Subsequently, the airplane impacted right of the runway and sustained substantial damage to the right wing and fuselage. The pilot reported that there were no preaccident mechanical malfunctions or failures with the airplane that would have precluded normal operation.[8]

> Courtesy: National Transportation Safety Board

With some of these forms, there is space for the pilot to diagram the flight path, even focusing attention on the specific diagram of the area in which the incident occurred. The report associated with the above example includes video of the event from the airport's cameras as well as photos of the damage to the aircraft.

In many cases, a more detailed investigation occurs subsequent to the initial reporting of the event, and NTSB will publish the more extensive report. This report is very technical in nature, including details of events before the incident occurred, pilot and crew training and qualifications, condition of the aircraft, actions of all involved, analyses of conditions, and simulations of options that one could have taken to minimize the potential for the accident (which was probably considered a crisis as it happened) that occurred. Interviews with any crew members are involved, if possible—each representing a descriptive narrative of the event. At the end of the report, several recommendations about changes to training or equipment or flight actions are provided. After publication, the report contributes to an evaluative narrative or prescriptive narrative, depending on subsequent events.

An example of such a report is the investigation of the 2009 US Airways flight 1549 ditching into the Hudson River. Most people are aware of this incident as the flight captained by Chesley (Sully) Sullenberger that encountered a flock of birds, causing engine failure and a need to land quickly, with the captain choosing to set the plane down in the river after quickly evaluating a few options. The pilot's actions were subsequently recognized as heroic. A movie dramatizing the event and related investigation, including some fictionalization, was released in 2016.

As part of the investigation into the incident, each crew member was interviewed. These interviews were documented in a separate report, among several such reports. The particular report is 33 pages long, and the interview with Sullenberger occupies 14 pages. It should be noted that the interview was in-person and included multimodal elements not captured in the report itself. Consider the following portion of the first full page of that interview:

> He said both engines were heavily damaged and they were unable to maintain altitude at all. There was no relight; they were out of the envelope and were sinking rapidly. He saw the river, started APU and said they "were going to land in the Hudson." His focus became on outside and the speed tape. He was intent on maintaining wings level. He made a PA, "Brace for impact." He planned a touchdown next to a vessel. He called for flaps 2, and there was no time for anything else. He began to flare and maintained full aft stick through touchdown. He said the touchdown was not too bad.[9]

The final NTSB report itself (over 200 pages long) includes many items similar to the one characterized above. Generally, most of the report is descriptive and evaluative narrative. However, it includes prescriptive narrative with its recommendations. Relatively early in the report an initial recommendation is acknowledged:

> As a result of the US Airways accident, on October 7, 2009, the NTSB issued Safety Recommendation A-09-112 to the FAA to address the potential safety consequences of an air traffic controller not knowing the location of an airplane experiencing an emergency. Safety Recommendation A-09-112 asked the FAA to do the following: Modify [FAA] radar data processing systems so that air traffic controllers can instruct the systems to process the discrete transponder code of an aircraft experiencing an emergency as if it were an emergency transponder code.[10]

Later in the report, 25 recommendations are issued to the Federal Aviation Administration (FAA), with additional recommendations issued to two other agencies. These recommendations specify changes in protocol, practices, and policies.

The report includes a transcript of flight recorder information, including communication between air traffic controllers and the pilot. That transcript itself acts as a narrative of the event as it occurred. The report, with recommendations, acts as a prescriptive narrative for airlines and policy makers.

In each of the aircraft-related examples, note the use of specialized terms. Each is written for an audience knowledgeable about flight concepts and protocol. Further, the transcription of communication between pilots of the US Airways flight and air traffic controllers as well as the reporting of crew member interviews would not capture the multimodal attributes of the communication and interviews such as volume, rate, and inflection of voice as well as nonverbal cues expressed on their faces. The voice recorder would capture vocal elements of tone, rate, and volume as the crisis occurred and the plane landed in the river and was evacuated. Also, the voice recorder may include voice characteristics associated with the pilot's public announcements to the passengers such as tone, rate, and volume. Video footage shows passengers evacuating the plane and waiting for rescue from nearby boats.

A video recording of any interviews would show nonverbal elements of the messages as well as voice characteristics. Finally, such a video recording would also show body movements—hand and arm gestures—as crew members responded to questions and provided their own narrative of the event.

Because each recording is from a real event, pilots would experience mirroring as they read the narratives. Pilots could recall their own experiences in similar or nearly similar incidents, and the successful outcome of their experience with the situation and reading the narratives of others—whether successful or not (potential for engaging reward neurons)—would inform decision-making in the future. Further, specific recommendations—suggestions for changes to policy and/or practices—would come from reflection and consideration of how to remove or minimize potential for such risks or crises in the future.

Discussion

Find an incident report from any of the following fields online and note identified safety-risk themes: air travel, health care, construction, or engineering. Note any specialized terms used and the target audience's expected understanding of them. Review the report for some features of the characteristics identified by Menon and Rainer mentioned previously:

- The story must be an accurate model of the engineering problem.
- The story and any engineering solution to the problem should not be mixed in the presentation.
- Metaphors and assumptions within the story should be well-understood and, so far as possible, parallel the details of the engineering problem.
- The story must contain an element of drama, such as the potential for a fatal outcome for one or more characters.

CHAPTER 5

Risk Communication

A risk scenario occurs when there is potential for an undesirable event or outcome to occur, but it has not yet occurred. Risk can be considered relative to the likelihood of the occurrence of an event or outcome and its severity; that is, how likely is it to occur at all, and how bad is its impact likely to be? The COVID pandemic was in full force in the United States by mid-March of 2020; however, media and health professionals were talking about its potential likelihood of entering the United States and its possible impact as early as January of that year. Other countries had experienced various levels of the pandemic's impact, and officials were concerned about its spread within the United States. While many anticipated a high likelihood that it would appear in the United States, no one was talking about mask mandates, social distancing, or business closures at the time; its impact was considered to be low. The message, broadly, was one of "be aware."

About 10 years prior to COVID's rise, another highly transmittable virus was spreading across the country—H1N1. The most dramatic change people experienced with that, though, involved encouragement to wash or sanitize hands regularly, which was more of a tolerable inconvenience than an assault on civil rights. So, many recalled that experience and anticipated that sanitizing hands would be needed again. While COVID was highly transmittable, its impact generally was moderate in terms of placing unusual demands on individuals, hospitals, and healthcare. However, the risk of severe effects of COVID were not understood yet. U.S. authorities were aware of its impact in other countries, but the impact that it could have on the United States was not ascertained. Until it began spreading quickly in the United States, it was considered a low risk.

By late February 2020, not only were there documented cases in several states in the United States, but there was a surge of people needing to be hospitalized, and many victims were dying within days or a few weeks of exposure to it. These developments led many to understand that the likelihood of its spread and impact had risen to that of high risk. It was now likely to spread to almost all states, and its effect on individuals' health and the healthcare system could be severe. Once mid-March arrived, it was at a crisis stage, forcing the federal and state governments to implement several actions and policies that would change everyone's behaviors.

As mentioned in a previous chapter, our brains respond to risk by immediately considering the threat the risk poses to our self-preservation. As mentioned there, Schmalzle et al.[1] found that neural responses were most closely associated with the audience's emotional concerns and pain. If a possible event or outcome is identified as low risk, the emotional response is one of awareness but lack of action—the change to our usual habit or behavior is nominal—very low. Once the event or outcome is perceived to be of a higher risk, the emotional response is greater—genuine fear increases, and we have a sense that a larger change to our routine may be necessary. When the risk level increases to one of certainty, we know that we have to take action and change our behaviors. If we have experienced a similar change associated with a risk before, we are able to make the adjustment readily. If we have not experienced a similar adjustment, we do not know how we may respond to such change.

When we experience events that affect us negatively, we try to avoid them in the future, or we revert to the way we addressed the event or situation to respond to a similar situation. Again, many may have recalled merely having to sanitize their hands frequently during the H1N1 pandemic, which was a small change to one's habits. Many probably thought that sanitizing their hands would be the only change necessary in response to COVID. However, as case numbers rapidly grew and the severity was understood, and with the data reporting significant rises in hospitalizations and deaths, the level of risk increased dramatically. The situation went from risk to crisis within only two months. Consequently, the pandemic did not give organizations and audiences in the United States much time to understand what changes might be necessary to address it, complicating any implementation of changes.

One element that was common as the pandemic spread, however, was the stories those who were affected shared. Again, the narratives helped the general public understand the impact the virus was having, even if people did not yet understand how to respond. Golden, Krimski, and Plough[2] assert the link between the positive effects that those kinds of narratives have on audiences when dealing with technical information. The scientific data has some impact on the public's understanding the risk or crisis, but the personal stories that include specific actions move audiences to action more so than just the data.

Audiences are able to relate to personal stories connected to the technical or scientific phenomenon. Additionally, Malecki et al. note that, "even when factual information about a hazard is provided, the public perception of risk from an unknown and emerging hazard such as COVID-19 leads to a more emotional response or outrage... Therefore, outrage factors shaping public risk perceptions are important for clinicians to understand, because they will determine how and why the general public will react and respond to messages."[3] So, technical experts as well as managers planning a message must consider that what a particular audience "perceives as acceptable or unacceptable risk includes both the nature of the hazard and degree of outrage."

This risk narrative can take the form of third-person abstraction about what could happen or what symptoms one might experience relative to the event or issue associated with the risk. For example, with instructions, it is generally understood that a safety tip should be included if there is risk of potential harm connected to a given step or the entire operation/task. Instructions would include a "caution" if the potential harm involves a small inconvenience or minor injury, perhaps requiring only first aid. However, a "warning" would signal that the potential harm or injury is much greater than that associated with "caution." The narrative of the safety tip could include a statement about what specifically could happen and what precautions to take to minimize the risk. This may be somewhat an abstraction rather than a detailed experience. However, the information allows the reader to visualize an experience associated with the risk.

An example of this narrative is the information posted in the Website Vehicle History when Ford issued a recall of some of its 2020 Escape vehicles. The particular recall involved a safety element related to the seats; the vehicle had been manufactured with only two pawls—a device that facilitates manual adjustment of the seat. According to federal guidelines, vehicles that have manual seat adjustment should have three pawls. In the posting on the website, it is noted that: "With the third pawl missing from a manual seatback, it increases the chances that the seatback will fail in a crash. This means that the seat—and the person in it—might not be in the proper location for the airbags to protect them in a crash."[4]

The second sentence in that passage contains the risk narrative; given their experience of riding in a vehicle and understanding where airbags tend to be located, one can imagine an accident in which they would not be helped by airbags because the seat was not positioned properly relative to those locations. Perhaps the seat is too low for an airbag to prevent one from hitting the lower part of the dashboard.

Regarding the risk level, the posting went on to suggest that the risk was actually low for the Escape; "The good news is that the design flaw was discovered in August of 2019 before very many of the 2020 Ford Escape vehicles had even made their way to dealerships. If you happen to own a 2020 Ford Escape, there's almost no chance that this recall will affect your vehicle."[5] However, it also noted that the flaw was included on several other Ford vehicles prior to it being identified on the Escape. So, Escape owners could somewhat relax and consider when their vehicle was shipped to dealers.

The Role of Communicating Risk

Because of the varying levels of risk associated with an event or outcome, communication's primary role in conveying risk is to acknowledge that a possible negative event or outcome may occur. Doing so gives audiences a chance to become aware of the potential need to modify their behaviors at some point, while reassuring them that the organization is taking action to address the situation and minimize audience impact. Making the audience aware of a potential situation gives it time to transition and adjust emotionally to the potential change; change is much more difficult if it has to be implemented on very short notice. A transition period helps to accept change.

Further, communication of risk should acknowledge the risk level, any related data—for example, data related to a trend that may impact the audience, and possible behavior changes the audience may need to take. The more concrete this information is, the better. For example, a model statement may take the form of:

> We are aware that [x event/outcome] may occur, as it seems to be impacting [y markets/organizations/industries] in recent weeks in these ways [data showing trend in z]. We believe the risk to be low at this time, and we are [taking steps] to address it. We want [audience] to be aware that they may need to [action to change behaviors] if the risk increases. We will keep [audience] informed of changes in the level of that risk as we become aware of it.

As the risk level changes, the organization should make announcements updating any further information to help the audience understand how likely behavior change may be needed and when it may be implemented. Again, risk communication should facilitate transition to a different behavior or mindset while conveying as much detail as possible to help the audience understand specific changes that may be needed.

Example Case

The onset of the COVID-19 virus and the related pandemic provides an ideal case study in risk, crisis, and change communication. The phenomenon unfolded with examples of risk communication (pre-March 10, 2020), crisis communication (mid-March 2020–Fall 2020), and change communication (late March 2020–Summer 2021). The federal and state governments began a series of briefings to the public on the growing risk in the United States in early 2020. We will consider examples from the state of Ohio's series for rhetorical analyses applying the leadership communication and neuroscience concepts described in the first two chapters of the book and in subsequent chapters.

On February 27, 2020, Ohio's governor, Mike DeWine's office sent a news release announcing how the state was preparing for the potential arrival of the COVID-19 virus in the state and action it was taking at that time. Quoted remarks from both Mike DeWine and Amy Acton, the Director of the Ohio Health Department, were included in the message. The news release acknowledged that there were no documented cases of COVID-19 in the state yet but that they were communicating with various departments about action plans.

The message declares:

> "I want to be clear that the threat of Coronavirus in Ohio and the United States remains low," said Governor Mike DeWine, "but this could change, and we have to be prepared. I believe it is imperative that we are open with the public and are communicating information in real-time about the Coronavirus to both inform and educate our communities. We will communicate what we know, when we know it."

The message provided a listing of eight different actions the governor's office was taking, most of which involved communicating with various state agencies about risks and responses. The information directed at workers and others with which they worked related to sanitizing hands and areas of common gathering as well as guidance to higher education administrators to take action related to students, especially those traveling. The message does not detail specific biological makeup of the virus; it speaks to the actions the government was taking to address the risk.

Further, Dr. Acton stated, "Since the start of this outbreak, we've taken a proactive approach to prepare and carefully monitor potential cases and travelers about COVID-19 in Ohio." The message ends with a quoted passage attributed to Acton: "As this situation evolves, we will continually update Ohioans through our website, odh.ohio.gov, our Facebook page and our Twitter account."[6]

The press release illustrates some of the principles identified in previous chapters regarding setting up a potential event and informing the public of initial steps the state is taking to be proactive. While conveying risk, it reassures the public that the risk, at this time appears to be low. That helps to allay potential fears generally, and the acknowledgment of sanitizing hands frequently allows the public to anticipate action similar to what it experienced about 10 years before with the H1N1 pandemic.

Both of these strategies appeal to the audience's level of fear (low) and recollection of a previous experience (mirror neurons associated with a moderate change to behavior). The audience understands what the behavior entails and generally can accept that change.

In identifying specific actions that the state is taking, the message conveys a sort of narrative relative to preparing for the potential event. The public understands that such communication is necessary, but it is not directly affected by the communication to various departments beyond the encouragement to sanitize hands and places. This facilitates a transition phase in case further action is necessary.

People tend not to like having to make lots of changes at one time, especially without forewarning. Easing into change is more readily accepted; so, the message generally facilitates that. If anything, as we now know, it seems to understate the potential impact, suggesting that all of the steps it is taking should address most issues if the virus spreads to Ohio. Nevertheless, it includes a statement reassuring the public that further announcements will come as needed, suggesting that more action may be necessary.

A problem with the statement is that it does not specifically state what action individuals may need to take if the risk increases. Again, many probably inferred that the experience would be like what they experienced with the H1N1 virus, and that may have been what the government agencies thought, too. So, it was difficult to specify beyond that level.

The statement is in written form; so, one cannot consider multimodal elements of the message. However, a public audience may have seen news stories about the early cases that may have included images of people being treated at a hospital. However, because no one fully understood the risk, such an audience may not have responded meaningfully to the images.

Chapter Summary

Risk communication should include the following attributes:

1. Acknowledge the anticipated event/outcome and level of risk (likelihood of occurring as well as impact) by stating trends with related data.

2. Consider the audience's background with specialized terminology and limit or remove technical language while emphasizing information the audience will understand easily—actions to take or symptoms of a problem.

3. Indicate what action(s) the organization is taking to try to address the situation.

4. Specify what action(s) the audience may need to take if the risk increases.

5. Compare the situation or risk to a previous situation or event with which the audience may have experience or of which it has awareness.

6. Try to estimate and convey when the risk could become a crisis.

7. Convey that any updates will be provided as related information becomes clear.

8. Try to mirror the audience in any way possible.

Such announcements should include narratives as well as numeric data so that the audience can make connections between the data and what they might need to do. However, considerable sensitivity is required to ensure information the audience will understand—data (technical audience) versus narrative about actions to take (less technical audience).

Risk Communication Case Activities

Two case studies are provided in this section that provide for practice in the analyses of risks. For the most part, in a technical risk setting such as a product recall, one hopes that potential mechanical issues that could impact the performance of the product and its safety can be identified before anyone suffers a serious accident or event from that issue.

Information about the situation and the messages addressing it is provided. As you review the information in each case, consider neural elements that may be affected by the phrasing of the message, using the previous case examples as a model.

Mercedes-Benz: Braking

In June of 2022, Mercedes-Benz issued a recall of almost one million vehicles globally—SUVs and luxury minivans—due to possible brake failure from corrosion. The recall indicated that models from several years were affected (2004–2015), but it did not indicate that there were any accidents associated with the problem. The message suggested that the problem may have been identified from several reports from technicians/mechanics about their observations when doing other repair work on the affected models. Consequently, this may be considered communication of risk rather than crisis. Note also that the risk is identified via narratives relating to technicians' observations during normal maintenance servicing. We do not have access to specific reports; however, it is very likely that those included technical language appropriate for the internal audience.

Several reports of the recall were posted online within days of the recall, each reporting different portions of the announcement from Mercedes-Benz. Here is a compilation of the different portions of the statement issued by Mercedes-Benz from a sampling of those reports:

> After extended time in the field and in conjunction with signifi-cant water exposure, this corrosion might lead to a leakage of the

brake booster. The problem could lead to "an increase in the brake pedal forces required to decelerate the vehicle and/or to a potentially increased stopping distance."[1]

According to Eddy, "Mercedes said it was recalling the cars for inspection, and had no way of knowing exactly how many would have corrosion damage."[2] According to France-Presse, Mercedes-Benz also acknowledged that:

> "Mercedes-Benz confirmed the recall in a statement to the AFP news agency, stating the move was based on "analysis of isolated reports for certain vehicles."
>
> "In rare cases of very severe corrosion, it might be possible for a particularly strong or hard braking maneuver to cause mechanical damage to the brake booster, whereby the connection between brake pedal and brake system would fail," Mercedes said.
>
> "In such a very rare case, it would not be possible to decelerate the vehicle via the service brake. Thus, the risk of a crash or injury would be increased."[3]

Further, Hurd stated that, "Mercedes says early signs of failure include a soft brake pedal or audible signs of air in the braking system (sucking, hissing or wheezing noises from the pedal are potential indicators of contaminated brake fluid)."[4]

With each announcement, note that no technical detail is offered; however, symptoms of the problem and when it may be noticeable are provided within a narrative form describing in what form a symptom may appear during operation of the vehicle.

From this set of passages, one can analyze the complete message relative to application of neuroscientific elements and narratives.

Case Questions

1. How might this be used as an evaluative narrative? Prescriptive narrative?
2. Have you ever experienced mechanical problems with a vehicle that were part of a general recall? Describe your experience (create a narrative)?

3. Identify ways that the speaker tries to mirror their audience in their words, narrative, or visually.

4. How might the audience be able to perceive mirroring with the speaker either in their words, narrative, or visually (response to this may not be same as that for 2)?

5. Identify specific narratives used by the speakers and how members of the audience could relate to them.

6. Has the speaker conveyed trustworthiness? How/how not?

7. How could the speaker improve their message relative to engaging mirror neurons?

8. How could the speaker improve their message by engaging reward neurons?

Cryptocurrency—Investment Risks

Investing in stocks, bonds, and other financial products involves learning about and understanding benefits and drawbacks inherent in the investment markets. Professional investors need to take several courses and pass professional licensure examinations before they can make investment decisions for other people. Most individual investors will do considerable research to understand how stocks and other investment products work. Stock and commodities investors expose themselves to a range of risks when they engage in various forms of investment. Generally, these are well known and repeated in financial management-related textbooks and in finance-related sources online.

The most commonly identified risks include volatility of economic markets and putting all of one's money into a single stock or financial product or very few stocks or products. Economic markets are changing frequently and can fluctuate dramatically on short notice. Thus the risk associated with such volatility is that one may purchase an investment vehicle based on what they understand to be reliable information and still lose money if they sell during an economic downturn or when a crisis negatively affects the company's or investment vehicle's value. The risk of placing too much trust (and money) in one stock/vehicle is that if that company's or vehicle's value declines, the investor will lose a lot of money.

Even as they identify the risks, experts always provide tips on how to minimize risks. The best way to address both of the risks mentioned here is to diversify and plan for long-term investing. If an individual wants to monitor the market on a frequent basis and does not mind changing course often, they can try to sell off stock or products when they are at a high value and buy at a lower price. Also, diversification—buying several different investment products—can balance any losses from certain stocks, for example, with gains from others. Again, these strategies are included in training for investment professionals and are available to serious private, individual investors; complex investment decisions require technical understanding of financial markets and investment vehicles.

A more recent financial product included these risks and general tips to minimize risk, and it brought a few more risks with it. Cryptocurrency (currency based on digital assets or "coins") became a real financial product in 2009, and, by 2022, several billions of dollars had been invested into various cryptocurrencies. Many of these were priced very high, with one Bitcoin—the most popular form of cryptocurrency—being worth just under US$68,000 in November 2021.[5] If one had purchased five Bitcoins in July 2017—at the price of US$1970, that investment of less than US$10,000 would have been worth US$340,000 in November 2021. However, the price of Bitcoins was more volatile than was the market generally; this was good when the price rose and bad when the price fell. For example, in early June 2022, that same investment of five Bitcoins was worth just over US$150,000. That crash was linked to another kind of cryptocurrency that was involved in a crisis (more on that in the crisis communication exercises). So, the risk to investors was related to market volatility, as mentioned before. The value of a financial product can change quickly, and this potential was magnified with most decentralized cryptocurrencies.

A few cryptocurrencies were labeled as "stable coins," which meant that their price/value was tied to the U.S. dollar such that one stable coin would be worth US$1. The price would move with the value of the dollar. As such, while volatile, it was considered much less risky than other cryptocurrencies. Nevertheless, it brought with it the other kinds of risks generally associated with cryptocurrencies.

As previously mentioned concerning the price fluctuations in Bitcoin, many personal stories of investors going from "rags to riches" were posted online. For example, Shnurenko[6] lists 10 such people, some of whom were teenagers when they made their first million dollars as cryptocurrency investors. There are also stories of people who lost money as the price dropped. These stories provided narratives that encouraged some to invest blindly into cryptocurrencies while cautioning others about the generally speculative nature of such an investment. Regardless, investors had to learn about the additional risks of these financial products as they considered investing in them.

Bybit Learn is one such source for identifying risks associated with cryptocurrencies. The website provides a good overview of various elements of cryptocurrency investing ranging from what cryptocurrencies are to how they might be used (some people use cryptocurrency as a form of payment where such currency is accepted while others use it strictly as an investment tool). The site also includes a section on many of the risks and how to minimize them. It opens its section on risks with the statement that, "[p]rofitable cryptocurrency trading requires a lot of time, experience, and technical skills to perfect. To avoid losing money, traders must make sensible choices and be aware of the possible risks."[7]

As it lists each risk, it describes the nature of the risk using relatively abstract terms often found in financial investing literature. For example, as it identifies volatility as a risk, it also states, "How to mitigate the risk: Only trade what you can afford to lose,…" Further, in responding to the risk of investing in only one product: "How to mitigate the risk: Diversification is key whether you trade cryptos or hold them long term. That way, you can reduce the risk." As mentioned above, these are standard tips for the two most common risks with any investment product. However, it also lists some not-so-common risks particular to cryptocurrencies.

One less common risk associated with cryptocurrency is "loss of private key." Cryptocurrencies are stored in digital form, and one needs to have a digital bank account that would have its own password or "key" to access it. If an investor loses that key (forgets the password), they cannot access the digital funds. It would be like losing the key to a bank safe deposit box and not being able to access whatever was in that box—ever. So, Bybit states, "If you lose your private key or your device where you store cryptocurrencies crashes, your assets may be at risk. Be sure to take the necessary precautions. How to mitigate the risk: To avoid such a scenario, create backup copies of the private key beforehand and keep them in a safe place."[8]

Another kind of risk is that of thieves hacking into a currency exchange and stealing "coins." Bybit alerts viewers of this and provides a particular narrative to illustrate the impact that it can have:

> Although security has significantly improved generally in the industry over the years (with increasingly sophisticated security measures being implemented), there have nevertheless been instances of exchanges being hacked in the history of crypto. A notable example is the infamous Mt. Gox hack of 2014, which at the time was the world's biggest Bitcoin exchange. Hackers stole around $460 million worth of Bitcoin.

Bybit notes a few other risks in investing in cryptocurrencies, but this information provides readers with enough information to assess the site. Again, consider the technical language used in some of these narratives while also considering the impact of rags-to-riches narratives. Such narratives make it seem easy to make money despite risks, encouraging many with little training to pursue risky investments. The "riches-to-rags" narratives may offer some balance.

Case Questions

1. How might this case be used as an evaluative narrative? A prescriptive narrative?
2. What research into new products or experiences have you done prior to making the purchase or participating in the experience? What risks were identified and how did you address them (create a narrative)?
3. Identify ways that the speaker tries to mirror their audience in their words, narrative, or visually.
4. How might the audience be able to perceive mirroring with the speaker either in their words, narrative, or visually (response to this may not be same as that for 3)?
5. Identify specific narratives used by the speakers and how members of the audience could relate to them.
6. Has the speaker conveyed trustworthiness? How/how not?
7. How could the speaker improve their message relative to engaging mirror neurons?
8. How could the speaker improve their message by engaging reward neurons?

CHAPTER 6

Crisis Communication

Heath and Millar define a crisis as "an untimely but predictable event that has actual or potential consequences for stakeholders' interests as well as the reputation of the organization suffering the crisis."[1] They go on to characterize a crisis as an extraordinary event that results in instability with a potentially negative outcome and creates a high level of media interest and scrutiny. A crisis can come in the form of an all-out change in the operating environment such as unstable stock market, or it can come from rumor or misinformation that may be untrue or inaccurate. Regardless, the organization has to spend time and resources to address the situation.

Heath and Millar identify three phases of a crisis, each bringing its own communication challenges: before the crisis happens, during the crisis, and after it has ended. Before the crisis occurs, the organization can acknowledge an anticipated issue that may affect its performance and let stakeholders and the public know that it is taking action to avoid the crisis or mitigate its impact on the organization. During the crisis, the organization must respond to audiences' concerns with reassurance that the impact is minimal and temporary. After the crisis has ended, the organization needs to reassure internal and external audiences that it is recovering and how it plans to avoid similar crises in the future. In all cases, the organization can use narrative to help control the situation, for a crisis creates a narrative, and the organization can control that narrative.

Indeed, Heath and Millar identify several attributes of a story and related analysis associated with a crisis: scene, characters, plots, and themes.[2] Within the narrative, the organization adopts a certain style, much of which reflects attributes of commonly identified characteristics of leadership communication: it should demonstrate concern, empathy, and compassion; it should be oriented toward solutions while conveying confidence; and it should show openness to input from stakeholders.[3] Most of these involve emotional intelligence.

While reviewing the link between emotional intelligence, narrative, and neuroscience from the first chapter of this book, recall that Caruso and Salovey describe the process of using emotions effectively in conveying messages:

1. Understand the situation, including the people involved.
2. Identify feelings of those involved.
3. Describe the focus of attention.
4. Understand emotions: why people feel a certain way about the focus of attention.
5. Manage feelings of those involved.[4]

Recall, also, that Bradberry and Greaves provided conceptualization of relationship-building connected to trust. Consider their tips for developing trustworthiness and the link to those attributes identified by Caruso and Salovey: Avoid giving mixed signals ("consistency in words, action, behaviors over time,"[5] accept feedback graciously, acknowledge others' emotions, and explain decisions.[6]

Zak conducted experiments to understand links between narratives that integrated emotional appeals, and he states, "my experiments show that character-driven stories with emotional content result in a better understanding of the key points a speaker wishes to make and enable better recall of these points weeks later."[7] People like to hear stories about others with connections to experience with which they might relate—stories that include reflection of emotional reactions to the experience appeal to mirror neurons. The storyteller conveys their own humanity to the audience.

Mirror neurons are active as one observes activity that one wants to emulate, or with which one wants to assimilate.[8] Mirror neurons are involved in persuasion. An audience wants to mirror some aspect of the speaker, or the speaker may want to reflect some quality of the audience to identify more effectively with it.

Example Case Analysis

Moving from the risk situation presented in Chapter 5 (Ohio's Response to the COVID Pandemic), the pandemic quickly became a crisis. In March 2020, Mike DeWine, Governor of Ohio, appeared on television to announce several measures in response to the COVID-19 virus pandemic. Many of these measures would force people to change their behaviors in an effort to address a number of dynamics associated with the pandemic-related crisis. Individuals were getting sick with the virus at an increasing pace, and hospitals were unable to manage the influx of patients who were severely affected by the virus. The governor would appear on television frequently through the next several months, often with the public health director of Ohio, Amy Acton. Together, they announced data related to case numbers, measures to limit the crisis, reactions to measures, political moves opponents of those measures were taking, and how individuals could improve their chances of not catching the virus. With each appearance, Dr. Acton generally provided scientific data collected by her office, exhibiting several aspects of technical communication such as data on the increase in the number of people infected and hospitalized. Eventually, this role shifted more to the governor.

Governor DeWine, though, in addition to talking through some basic updates, used occasional narratives about his own family's experiences as they limited family gatherings. Such narratives were meant to appeal to the audience, which was having similar experiences and frustrations to those that he described. He had to practice the policies that the administration had implemented. There are neuroscientific benefits for using narratives in such a rhetorical way—to persuade people to change their behavior and address a crisis. Narratives can help to establish ethos as well as a pathetic connection with the audience. They help the speaker connect with their audience by mirroring the audiences' experiences and sharing emotions they experience; these stimulate mirror neurons, helping the public relate to the governor and vice versa through shared narratives. Further, because there were frequent televised updates, multimodal rhetoric elements were also in play.

Science Versus Nonscience

Dr. Acton's presentations during the televised sessions added a certain kind of credibility to the information presented. Certainly, as a public health expert, the audience could likely trust that her data was accurate and the decisions she was making were out of an abundance of caution. Malecki et al.,[9] and Fiske, Cuddy, and Glick[10] note that the public responds favorably relative to trusting scientific information when it is reported by subject matter experts. As such, Acton served well to represent the scientific, technical reporting. Never did she use a personal narrative as she reported the data.

DeWine, though, had to represent the nonscience public and somehow show that he was close to the public. He was involved in the decision-making process associated with the measures and restrictions placed on the public and businesses. He had to demonstrate that his life had been impacted by the policies just as the general public's life had been affected so that the audience could see that his sacrifices mirrored many of theirs. In several of the presentations, he alluded to his position as a father and grandfather; he had not been able to see his children and grandchildren, except through Zoom; and he conveyed his own frustration with not being able to be with them.

Narrative and Change Neuroscience

A growing number of researchers and practitioners are finding the value of using narratives to encourage and facilitate change. Several scholarly articles on the subject have been published since the early 2000s, many since 2015. As noted earlier, Jeff Bezos, CEO of Amazon, prefers to use a narrative text that leads to discussion rather than use PowerPoint slides shows.[11] Saltmarsh states that narrative, "enables the possible to feel probable in ways our rational minds can't comprehend. When it comes to changing the values, mindsets, rules, and goals of a system, story is foundational."[12]

Saltmarsh goes on to indicate that a story helps to establish community and empathy—engaging emotional intelligence. She states, "[w]e can use story to create immersive scenarios of the future that engage people on an emotional and intellectual level. This work can make the possible feel more probable, bring new perspectives that challenge the goals and mindsets of a system, and enable the transformation of rules and processes."

This is echoed by Flynn,[13] who notes that studies have found that viewers who watched a documentary on mental illness changed their perception of mental illness more readily than those who watched a fictional show about it, even though both shows were about the same issues. The more real the story is the more it affects perception of reality and makes the prospects of change feel less threatening.

As we considered previously,[14] mirror neurons are active when someone observes activity they want to emulate or which they want to assimilate. Mirror neurons are involved in persuasion. An audience wants to mirror some aspect of the speaker, or the speaker may want to reflect some quality of the audience to assimilate with it more. In times of crises, audiences want to know that leaders understand their emotions and position and can demonstrate compassion. Reinforcing some attributes of Carosey and Salovey's emotional intelligence theory, Coatney explains that audiences assess how trustworthy a hopeful narrative may be relative to how compassionate the speaker appears.[15]

In November 2020, Governor DeWine appeared to announce a specific narrative about how he and his family were going to celebrate Thanksgiving while practicing the kinds of restrictions policy had placed on the public to minimize the virus's spread. Throughout, he speaks of their plan to use Zoom to facilitate some social interaction while not being together, perhaps trying to lead by example; that is, he describes how other families could use a digital videoconferencing tool to interact safely with each other. He essentially provides alternative guidelines for others to use but presents it as a narrative positioning his wife and himself as parents/grandparents who want to be with their family but understand the need for distancing. DeWine's wife, Fran, indicated that she would still cook the meal, and she acknowledged that she and her husband would drop off meals and then visit virtually, using Facetime and Zoom.

Golding, Krimsky, and Plough found through experiments that audiences generally responded more favorably to narratives related to experiences with a scientific phenomenon than to scientific data about that phenomenon.[16] Dahlstrom details this phenomenon in arguing for scientists to convey scientific information by including narratives.[17] Contrasting the usual "logical-scientific" approach to reporting technical information with narrative, he states that "logical-scientific and narrative communication are not just contrasting formats of communication, but represent two distinct cognitive pathways of comprehension." He goes on to state,

> Empirical studies support such a categorical difference between paradigmatic and narrative processing, and suggest that narrative processing is generally more efficient. Narratives are often associated with increased recall, ease of comprehension, and shorter reading times. In a direct comparison with expository text, narrative text was read twice as fast and recalled twice as well, regardless of topic familiarity or interest in the content itself.

Applying Hagle's[18] four specific attributes of hopeful narratives to the narrative analysis, one finds the following linkages:

1. Frame inspiring, long-term opportunity out in the future that can focus and motivate a large number of participants.

   DeWine calls attention to a desired outcome—fewer people getting sick with the virus, allowing more who do get sick to be able to find a hospital for attention.

2. Identify trends that suggest this opportunity is in fact becoming more achievable.

   DeWine and Acton explicitly show trends in cases—as they increase and as they decrease, suggesting how well vaccination and masking are working.

3. Identify obstacles and challenges that stand in the way of achieving the opportunity.

   More than once, DeWine acknowledged debate and disagreement about the mask and vaccine policies among, especially, Republican legislators and business owners. With each, he attempted to allay fears and use data/trends to show that policies were working and giving hope that the policies could be eased once a certain number of cases was reached.

4. Create an explicit call to action that will encourage people to come together and focus on increasing impact.

DeWine was explicit in his call to attend to and enforce the policies while also showing scientific data suggesting that the policies were working.

DeWine illustrated these points as well. In a recorded, motivational prelude to another session, he called on Ohioans to show unity in fighting the pandemic by placing United States and State of Ohio flags on their house, mentioning that his wife had just put one up on their house and that Dr. Acton's husband had put one up on their house, thus humanizing her and linking the science of the pandemic to the appeal for social unity. By calling for unity in fighting the pandemic's effects, the long-term outcome could be one in which people remain healthy, and it is through the restrictions that such an outcome can happen.

The Multimodal Considerations

Multimodal communication provides a richness beyond printed words. Beyond the narrative style, one can also see elements of dress, spatial positioning of people in the reports, and use of data within the rhetoric associated with the message. DeWine generally dressed as a professional politician—nice suit, dress shirt, and tie. Acton's dress emphasized a white coat—a very medical-like representation, distinguishing herself from others in the room as the medical/public health official.

As previously noted, Acton reported the scientific data regarding projections and existing trends, showing a slide show or standing near an easel with posters of data and graphics. This further connected her with the scientific elements of the report.

When DeWine included his wife in some messages, she was positioned next to him—as they represent a married couple, much as those members of the general public who are married may have perceived themselves as physically and emotionally close.

Conclusion

Through the hopeful narrative and multimodal dynamics associated with the messages, DeWine and Acton were able to accomplish an element of trustworthiness among the general public while assimilating with the public in a few ways. They engaged mirror neurons through that assimilation while appealing to reward neurons by using the hopeful narrative to suggest that a positive outcome—declining infections/hospitalizations and easing of restrictions—was possible. Again, technical terminology was limited, and prescriptive narratives of ways to respond or behave to limit the crisis's impact were offered.

Crisis Communication Case Activities

The two cases presented here provide practice in applying principles from the chapter to actual situations. The first at the time of this writing was evolving from an industry crisis to a possible criminal case. The second is a response to the spill of toxic chemicals from a train derailment.

USTerra Crash and "Stable Coin" Cryptocurrency

As mentioned previously within one of the risk communication exercises, cryptocurrency rose in popularity as a financial product in the 2010s such that several billions of dollars had been invested into cryptocurrencies by 2022. Let's review several points associated with cryptocurrency risks that led to a severe collapse and crisis for one such currency.

As noted before, many of cryptocurrencies were extremely volatile. Recall the example illustration from the earlier exercise: If one had purchased five Bitcoins in July 2017—at the price of US$1970, that investment of less than US$10,000 would have been worth US$340,000 in November 2021. Many understood this volatility, and cryptocurrencies had generally experienced good volatility—upward swings in value. However, a crisis occurred relative to a different kind of cryptocurrency that caused almost all cryptocurrencies to drop dramatically in value in May 2022.

You will recall that a few cryptocurrencies were labeled as "stable coins," which meant that their price/value was tied ("pegged" is the term that was used) to the U.S. dollar such that one stable coin would be worth US$1. Until 2025, the U.S. federal government tried to regulate cryptocurrencies but made no effort to back them as the U.S. dollar is backed. In 2025, the U.S. Congress put more effort into ascertaining vehicles by which to stabilize cryptocurrencies. Until then, because the price would move with the value of the dollar, such "stable coins" were considered much less risky than other cryptocurrencies. However, a risk that was never publicly identified prior to the crash—but noted in initial internal communications related to the coin's development—caused the extreme devaluation of the U.S. Terra coin—one such "stable coin."

U.S. Terra (UST) was created by Do Kwon as a stable coin in 2018 and integrated a complex algorithm to establish and maintain its value connection with the U.S. dollar. The "coin" was formally launched in 2020, and an organization called Luna Foundation Guard (LFG) was created in early 2022 to monitor the coin and secure digital (crypto) funds to guard against a potential crisis related to the algorithm. The foundation's guard "fund" would be called Luna; and, in simple terms, it would raise funds that could be used to keep the UST coin linked to the U.S. dollar using traditional macroeconomic principles of limiting or creating digital assets to support UST's valuation. Through April 2022, UST was able to maintain its US$1 "peg" with actions of LFG, but in early May, it began to lose that peg. On May 9, 2022, the "peg" with the U.S. dollar collapsed, and the coin was valued at 35 cents. Trading on the coin continued intermittently over the next three days—being stopped at times but allowed to resume periodically. By May 13, the coin's value had dropped to one cent.[1]

During its development, an analyst identified a concern about UST's viability as a stable coin. Cyrus.ismoney posted to Twitter internally about the concerns over the UST/Luna/Terra linkage. Simply put, if Terra were to fall, then "Luna would fall as investors would panic, and Terra would continue to fall, and then they would just each keep contributing to each other's demise. This is what happened to Nubits, like 3 years ago."[2] However, Do Kwon asserted in 2021 that such an event was not likely to occur.[3] Even as some questioned UST's stable coin model, Kwon challenged those statements, reassuring the public that the model would work. In early May, with the initial drop from the US$1 peg, Luna was able to return it back to the US$1 value, but then investors pulled out of Luna and UST—exactly what was predicted.

In the few days after the collapse of Luna and UST, several reports challenging Kwon's reputation and damaging trust in him were published.[4-6] Rather than respond immediately, though, he remained silent for several days.

On May 11, 2022, Kwon posted to Twitter his concern for the situation and a plan to address it. Mourya states,

Kwon's reappearance was accompanied by a review of the current situation and a proposal to mint more UST:

I understand the last 72 hours have been extremely tough on all of you—know that I am resolved to work with every one of you to weather this crisis, and we will build our way out of this.

Together.

— Do Kwon (@stablekwon) May 11, 2022

Proposal 1164 [a proposal submitted to the Terra community for a vote] addresses the slow burn of UST, the leading cause of the stablecoin's high supply and unstable peg. The proposal elaborates on the loss of confidence in the UST peg and coordinated attacks with the goal of UST de-peg and pushing Luna prices down aggressively.[7]

As one might expect, there was speculation that Kwon had profited somehow by the devaluation of the coins, but he responded that he had not.[8] Shortly after that, he had to respond to reports that he had evaded taxes in South Korea.[9] As investigations continued into 2023, he reported that he was not hiding, but he also did not acknowledge where he was. He was eventually arrested at an airport with fake travel documents trying to fly to a country that had no extradition treaty with the United States. As of early 2025, he is in U.S. custody and facing trial scheduled for 2026.

As observed with the series of responses and delayed responses, Kwon left himself open to much speculation and distrust. Consider how the series of events before and after the crisis, in particular, Kwon's statements and actions along the way, affect the perception of trust in Kwon among investors and the public. Even as the technical dynamics played out in the markets, the narratives of people who suffered were a strong influence on Congress's response.

Given how risky even "stable" coins proved to be, by early June of 2022, the U.S. Senate was considering legislation that would no longer allow algorithm-oriented stable coins and would force such cryptocurrencies to use non-digital assets to back them. As Quiroz-Gutierrez reported,

The bill, introduced on Tuesday by Sens. Cynthia Lummis (R-Wyo.) and Kirsten Gillibrand (D-N.Y.) dubbed the Responsible Financial Innovation Act, says that "payment stablecoins" must be backed by "not less than 100 percent of the face amount of the liabilities of the institution on payment stablecoins issued by the institution"...The bill defines "payment stablecoins" as digital assets that are redeemable on a one-to-one basis with the dollar or other legal tender, are issued by a business entity, are accompanied by a statement from the issuer that it is backed by one or more financial non-crypto assets, and are used as a medium of exchange.[10]

In this case, a little-known risk associated with cryptocurrencies turned into a crisis that forced legislative and practical change in the investment industry.

Case Questions

1. How can the communications within this case be used as prescriptive narrative?
2. Identify ways that the speaker tries to mirror their audience in their words, narrative, or visual presentation.
3. How might the audience be able to perceive mirroring with the speaker either in their words, narrative, or visual presentation (response to this may not be same as that for 2)?
4. Identify specific narratives used by the speakers and how members of the audience could relate to them.
5. Has the speaker conveyed trustworthiness? How/how not?
6. How could the speaker improve their message relative to engaging mirror neurons?
7. How could the speaker improve their message by engaging reward neurons?
8. Describe a crisis that you experienced (perhaps medical or financial). What happened? How did you understand it to be a crisis? What did you do about it? Did you have a friend/relative who had a similar experience and who shared it with you to help you understand what to do? Have you shared the experience with anyone; why?

East Palestine Train Derailment

Just before 9 p.m. local time on February 3, 2023, 50 cars of a train that included hazardous chemicals as cargo derailed in East Palestine, Ohio. Eleven of the cars contained such chemicals as vinyl chloride (highly volatile gas), ethyl acrylate, and isobutylene (both of which are toxic and potentially carcinogenic). Further investigation found that butyl acrylate, ethylhexyl acrylate, and ethylene glycol monobutyl ether were also involved. The derailment caused an explosion among several of the cars, and a fire burned for a few days.

Given the hazardous materials involved, local officials ordered residents in the area to evacuate due to potential for toxic contaminants in the air. Fire officials also started a "controlled" burn of a particular area to safely burn off the vinyl chloride. There were no injuries or deaths directly from the derailment; however, concerns over contaminants in the air and water persisted. Technical details were limited to potential threats if the materials were ingested or breathed in.

The train was operated by Norfolk Southern, and their first public response, about 10 days after the event, was to commit support and funding to help rebuild the community. Trying to convey sensitivity to the local community, Norfolk Southern's CEO stated,

> I hear you, we hear you. My simple answer is that we are here and will stay here for as long as it takes to ensure your safety and to help East Palestine recover and thrive... Crews are cleaning the site thoroughly, responsibly, and safely. Our Family Assistance Center is helping community members meet immediate needs. Together with local health officials, we have implemented a comprehensive testing program to ensure the safety of East Palestine's water, air, and soil. And we have established a $1 million community support fund as a down payment on our commitment to help rebuild.[1]

About three weeks after the event, federal officials opened a medical clinic in the town to support those residents who were experiencing symptoms of health effects from the fires. Again, technical information was limited, and the focus was on encouraging certain behaviors to minimize potential impact.

Over the course of the next several months, investigations into the cause found compromised wheel bearings on one of the cars that eventually failed, causing the axel of the car to fall apart. Further, Norfolk Southern announced additional funds to help with the community's recovery.

Pendelton has critiqued Norfolk Southern's initial crisis communication response, characterizing it as slow, impersonal, and mostly defensive. This initial response (first month) is critical to establishing trust in the company. Pendelton states, "Today, nearly a month after the derailment, it feels like Norfolk Southern's crisis machine has finally swung into full gear. But is it already too late?" Pendelton offers recommendations on how Norfolk Southern should have handled that initial response, incorporating visual effects:

> Instead of seating Shaw for questions, he should be seen in East Palestine's homes, shoulder-to-shoulder with EPA inspectors. He should walk property lines and kneel in unplanted gardens, sifting the dirt through his fingers. Convoys of Norfolk Southern trucks should be filmed bringing countless loads of fresh soil to town while company employees help school children plant a new community green space.[2]

Several lawsuits have been filed against Norfolk Southern, and the company has countered, trying to share blame with entities associated with the rail system and the company whose chemicals it was shipping. As of this writing (2025), these legal actions continue.

Case Questions

1. In what ways can the communications of this situation be considered as descriptive, evaluative, and/or prescriptive narratives?
2. Identify ways that the CEO tries to mirror their audience in their words, narrative, or visually.
3. How might the audience be able to perceive mirroring with the speaker either in their words, narrative, or visually?
4. Identify specific narratives the speaker could have used to relate to the residents.
5. How did the speaker try to convey trustworthiness?
6. How could the speaker improve their message relative to engaging mirror neurons?
7. How could the speaker improve their message by engaging reward neurons?

CHAPTER 7

Change Communication

The most challenging form of change is large-scale change. An organization, for example, might change its focus or try to rebrand itself to adjust to market forces, or a public official might seek to implement a new program that challenges the "status quo," or the "usual way" of doing things. Sometimes, certain technologies that facilitate much of the organization's work must change, affecting hundreds of employees as well as customers or consumers. Such major changes represent significant shifts in behavior and ways of operating for many and require different considerations beyond those we have identified previously. As we considered in Chapter 1, a risk is understood to require a small-scale change to behavior; we just have to be aware of the risk and how we can avoid or minimize the chances of it occurring. A crisis involves a greater challenge, but most understand that it is short-lived. Stakeholders may need to change their behaviors for a while, and that may be inconvenient, but will be able to return to usual behaviors at some point in the near future.

The examples presented so far, especially those related to the COVID-19 pandemic, illustrate such situations. As the risk of COVID's arrival in the United States increased, public health officials and other public officials acknowledged the threat, and how to address it, and what actions the public and various business entities should take to limit the spread. Initially, it was accepted as needed, but the longer it went on, greater inconvenience and more resistance occurred. Likewise, as the pandemic spread, the crisis associated with the rate of the spread and the inability of hospitals and health officials to keep pace with it and manage the case numbers brought with them a longer period of mask and vaccine-related policies. Healthcare experts used their technical and scientific knowledge and skills to work toward development of vaccines and to collaborate with public officials—experts in public policy—to create policies to manage the crisis while trying to limit the spread of illness and death. Resistance to these policies increased to the point of violent outbreaks at public meetings to protest mask mandates or urge mask safety. Even as experts disagreed among themselves, they had to communicate messages to one another, themselves, and to the public that included specialized terms, all while appealing to the general public's needs and concerns.

Recall from the chapter on crisis communication that Ohio's public health official and governor both described plans to use Zoom to facilitate family gathering during the Thanksgiving holiday. They were acting as role models for the public while sharing a prescriptive narrative that the general public could mirror.

However, the longer the pandemic-related policies lasted, the more inconvenient the "new normal" became. Eventually, safety policies were loosened as more people were vaccinated and as some people used masks without being forced to do so, understanding their responsibility for their own safety. In many areas, mask mandates gave way to mask-optional policies. Nevertheless, choosing to continue to wear a mask represented a genuine change for many.

Almost every industry experienced rapid change through the COVID-19 pandemic and its impact on the economy in general. The economic environment brought on by the pandemic and policies that were implemented to reduce or limit its impact—masks, social distancing, stay-at-home orders, and distinctions between "essential" and "nonessential" workers—dramatically changed much of the operating landscape. The changes it forced may be considered a once-in-80 years shift. Only major, worldwide pandemics and world wars have elicited the kinds of economic shifts like those experienced during the COVID-19 pandemic. Organizations that were relatively stable when the pandemic hit suffered, and organizations that were already in fiscal hardship collapsed.

Likewise, some businesses and public entities had to redesign workspaces to facilitate distancing and implement shields to limit the opportunity for the virus to spread. Clear screens appeared in restaurants, for example, and at cashier booths in stores. Many businesses and stores have maintained these even as masking and distancing policies have loosened. This represents a physical change for those businesses and workplaces.

While the changes may have felt awkward at first, they have become relatively accepted as people have become accustomed to them.

This experience with abrupt changes due to the health concerns of the pandemic raises the most important difference between risk communication, crisis communication, and change communication—allowing time to transition and, possibly, facilitating that change in phases. The two cases described in this chapter focus attention on large-scale technology-related changes at two organizations—a motor vehicle manufacturer and an institution of higher education. Each shows a needed commitment from many while also using some means of linking previous experience with certain similar processes or technologies to facilitate the transition.

General Motors (GM) Shift to Electric Vehicles (EV) (COVID Influenced)

As the COVID pandemic swept the United States, the federal government exercised wartime policies to stimulate production of materials and equipment that could address various shortages such as sanitizers and respiratory equipment—respirators (masks) and ventilators (artificial breathing device). Companies with manufacturing systems in place and that could easily convert to a needed product were now producing such items. One example of this shift was the move that GM—a vehicle manufacturing company—made to producing ventilators to help hospitals keep up with demand among patients who were having considerable difficulty breathing.

The virus brought on symptoms consistent with bronchitis and pneumonia, making breathing very difficult. Hospitals tended to have only a handful of ventilators in their stock, and a shortage of ventilators at all hospitals was part of the pandemic crisis. Manufacturers of ventilators could not produce more equipment fast enough. Because of its manufacturing prowess, GM changed some of its production facilities to enable it to help a west coast manufacturer increase production of ventilators. While it made this shift to address the crisis of the pandemic, as the pandemic moved to more of an endemic and more people were vaccinated against the virus, GM used this experience to shift to an aggressive mode for production of EVs.

In recent years, there had been a political movement among environ-mentalists and politicians to encourage less reliance on fossil fuels such as gasoline to move to more reliance on electric fuel options. Several ve-hicle manufacturers had already begun manufacturing EVs prior to the pandemic; and as more charging stations came into existence across the United States, more people felt better about buying EVs. Still, a large ma-jority of people bought gas-powered vehicles; so, demand for those was still high. Sensing a shift in U.S. culture and political pressure to reduce gas fuel emissions, GM used its experience with ventilator production to ramp up production of EVs. Krisher stated that,

> In March of last year, GM put hundreds of workers on the project to help Ventec Life Systems of the Seattle area ramp up its produc-tion at a time when there were fears that the country would run short of the breathing machines.
>
> GM put up capital and converted an electronics factory in Indiana to help make the ventilators with a speed that one supply chain expert said was "lightning fast."
>
> Barra [GM CEO] said the company now uses the same ap-proach for its own electric vehicles, software, and partially auto-mated driver-assist systems.[1]

In describing the ventilator manufacturing shift, Krisher notes that, ac-cording to Barra, "employees approached the problem as if their loved ones might need the breathing machines and accomplished the goal."[2] With the experience of producing ventilators at lightning speed, GM is building factories that can enable it to mass-produce EVs at a faster rate than was previously possible. This may help to reduce the cost of EVs and speed up a general shift among buyers to EVs.

In early 2021, CEO Barra began speaking more about GM's com-mitment to EVs and announcing a series of increased investments in that shift. Hawkins writes,

> GM has been trying to convince investors of its own commit-ment to electric vehicles. The company recently committed to spending $27 billion on electric and autonomous vehicles

through 2025—up from the $20 billion it announced before the COVID-19 pandemic. GM has also said it will launch 30 new electric vehicles around the world, more than two-thirds of which will be available in North America.[3]

The effort included a change in GM's logo, which Hawkins described:

> It's been about a decade since GM has last tweaked its logo, but this update represents the starkest change in the company's 113-year history. The most obvious change is the use of a lowercase "gm" in the logo, after previously only using capital letters. The underline has been shortened to just the "m," in a nod to the company's recently announced Ultium electric vehicle battery and platform.[4]

He, further, explains that it has a sort of smartphone app icon look to it.

The transition to EV production was introduced, further, by Barra as an all-inclusive effort, helping employees transition to the new production. According to LaReau, "Barra said GM is focused on bringing its current workforce along, while helping to build a diverse pipeline of talent…That means creating an environment where everyone feels valued, comfortable to be themselves and emboldened to do their best work. It also means including them in a transition to EVs."[5] LaReau quotes Barra as stating, "Whether they're an engineer or a teammate working on the assembly line in one of our plants, they need to know they are a part of our future. Our goal is, as we make this transition, we bring everyone along."[6]

While the announcements were generally hopeful and positive, Barra had to convey to shareholders the implications of these investments on the heels of a weak economy for vehicles generally. Garsten states that, "…Barra spoke of increased investments in the production and development of electric vehicles and battery, accelerating EV introductions and letting shareholders know all that spending means they won't be receiving dividends for the time being."[7]

Within the political climate of the period, EVs were increasingly popular alternatives to the standard combustion engine, eliminating much pollution. So, the political climate affected the audience's reaction as well.

Further, while few who were alive during WWII would be part of an audience, many recall the technological changes and increased capacities for production of vehicles just after WWII. So, narratives from that period could have helped audiences—technical and nontechnical—understand how the pandemic and political environment facilitated a shift to EV technologies.

Consider how the different audiences—the general public, employees of GM, and GM investors—might perceive the set of these statements in taking the company in a new direction and responding to the changing automotive environment.

Case Questions

1. Have you ridden in or test-driven an EV? Describe the experience and difference that you noted with driving a vehicle with a traditional combustion engine as if sharing with a friend or colleague who is considering such a purchase.
2. Identify ways that the speaker tries to mirror their audience in their words, narrative, or visually.
3. How might the audience be able to perceive mirroring with the speaker either in their words, narrative, or visually (response to this may not be same as that for 2)?
4. Identify specific narratives used by the speakers and how members of the audience could relate to them.
5. Have the speakers conveyed trustworthiness? How/how not?
6. How could the speakers improve their messages relative to engaging mirror neurons?
7. How could the speakers improve their message by engaging reward neurons?

LMS Technology-Related Change at KSU: General Shift and COVID Shift

Many school districts and institutions of higher education use a LMS to facilitate instruction and coursework. Instructors can use these to post instructional materials and assignments as well as schedules for various classwork. Students access them to review information as well as submit assignments. Instructors can grade assignment submissions in these systems as well and post results. Because of these various tools and uses, online classes tend to be facilitated through them, too. Two popular and competing—LMS products are Blackboard and Canvas. The companies that license them arrange contracts for use and support with institutions. After a decade of using Blackboard's LMS versions, Kent State University made the decision to switch to Canvas. Because of the varied pedagogical functions associated with different LMS products, this represented a substantial change in how class activities would operate, especially for those instructors and students using online delivery. Complicating the transition is that the early part of it occurred during the latter part of the COVID-pandemic period. I detail this transition here and offer analysis that includes consideration of multimodal elements, since much of the training related to the transition included video, documents that integrated graphics, and videoconferencing interactions.

The administration approached this change carefully. The university's contract to use Blackboard was due to end in 2019. Consequently, the university's technology committee began review of the system while considering two other systems—Canvas and Desire2Learn. Ultimately, the committee decided to survey faculty and students about their opinions on Blackboard as well as potential for using either of the other systems. Many students, for example, had experienced Canvas or Desire2Learn through their pandemic experience of remote learning during high school. So, part of the decision would include input from any willing to complete the survey.

Upon making the decision to change to Canvas, the university put together informational items to help faculty and students understand the new interface and how to use it. They also facilitated numerous online workshops, providing training of various features. Some of these items included showing how the Canvas interface was similar to Blackboard's interface and tools. Haas[8] and Norman[9] encourage the interface of new technologies to be as close as possible to existing tools they update or advance. This design allows for easier transition and use, thereby also facilitating quicker acceptance.

On page 4 of the "Canvas Blackboard Comparison: Instructor Guidebook," it is stated that, while Canvas tools are being identified and described, Blackboard tools related to each are identified for comparison purposes in parentheses. The first such reference is on the same page and related to creating assignments and how the assignment then appears in the LMS's grade system: "An assignment must be created to create a column in Grades (i.e.: Gradebook)." On the same page is a reference to the peer review tools in Canvas, which uses the term "Peer Review" to access those tools; in parentheses Blackboard's term is provided: "Self and Peer Assessments."[10] These help the reader relate the new LMS' tools back to their experiences with similar tools in the previous LMS. While the handbook emphasizes Canvas interface and tools, there are explicit references to Blackboard and similarities.

Further, the university decided to use a two-year period for the transition. Both systems would be available, and faculty would be able to use either, though faculty were encouraged to begin the transition. One of the more important factors related to change success is understanding how long it may take to change. Fenson states, "Many leaders and managers underestimate the length of time required by a change cycle. That's why numerous reports indicate poor performance following many IPOs, mergers, change initiatives, etc."[11] The timeline for the change needs to enable people to adapt emotionally as well as physically. Jim Raber, the executive director of Information Services, Educational Technology, and Service Management at Kent State University stated that, "As courses get built out, having faculty review the structure of their course and to re-think how content is laid out, … this is probably the biggest amount of work for them… It's not hard but requires effort." He went on to state that, "Changing LMS (Learning Management System) is a lot like moving houses. You move into a house, but it takes a little while to feel like home."[12]

Kent State made the announcement to transition to Canvas in 2020, began facilitating training sessions in mid-spring of 2021, and scheduled the end of Blackboard use for Summer of 2022. Training sessions included both video-recordings as well as live, synchronous, and interactive sessions. Even subsequent to full implementation, the university continued to provide technical support for faculty and students, continuing to make the training videos available.

These videos and live training sessions enabled viewers to experience information via multiple modes, seeing specific keystrokes were needed to access and use specific tools and navigate the course site. The ability to see and have some hands-on training before the shift occurred enabled faculty to easily transition to Canvas, drawing on previous experiences with Blackboard.

The COVID pandemic further complicated this technology shift. The first year of the transition was the 2020 to 2021 academic year. Almost all classes were still delivered remotely, meaning instructors had to use the LMS. A statistic that I was made aware of late in the pandemic period was that about 70 percent of classes offered before the pandemic were held in the classroom. This surprised me, because much of my teaching by then was online or facilitated through the LMS. The shift to the online environment brought on by COVID was easy for me because I had been in the environment for several years. For many faculty, though, it was their first time without a classroom as the primary contact with students. They may have provided some course materials via the LMS, but they had almost no experience teaching in that environment, either synchronously or asynchronously.

The university's IT and Educational Technologies offices stepped up training and facilitated additional equipment for faculty use; however, starting the shift to Canvas with all of the other technology-related challenges associated with teaching in the pandemic context increased stress for many. Nevertheless, the university did what it could to make the transition as easy as it could.

While prescriptive in nature, training associated with new technology should incorporate as much information connecting the new technology with previous technologies with which the audience has experience to allow the audience to understand how it mirrors their previous experience. The more the audience can connect their previous experience to the newer technology, the easier the change may seem.

Discussion

1. If you have been in a position of having to change a primary technology associated with your work), what steps did the organization offer to help with the transition? If you entered an organizational setting not having experienced its primary technologies, how did you learn those technologies?

2. How can the institution use this case experience as an evaluative or prescriptive narrative to support other changes in LMS technology used for teaching and learning? What points might engage some mirror neurons or reward neurons?

Change Communication
Case Activities

Case studies are provided in this section to allow practice in analyses of change related to crisis and general change. Information about the situation and the messages addressing it are provided. As you review the information in each case, consider neural elements that may be affected by the phrasing of the message, using the previous case examples as a model. Use Figure 3.1 rubric to organize your analysis:

State University of New York (SUNY) and COVID Response

As ordered by the various state and local governments during the COVID pandemic, people were required to use masks and try to "socially distance" (maintaining a six-foot separation from others) when going into public spaces. Many entities were either closed or moved to remote participation. This was the case with many public colleges and schools. New York had been adjusting to the spread of the pandemic in February 2020, and the first public college-related announcements related to responding to it were made in early March (recall that such announcements were being made in Ohio in mid-March—about a week later). Kristina Johnson, The SUNY Chancellor at the time, implemented several of the same kinds of policies that many other institutions did—including the change to remote delivery of instruction. At the end of the academic year, though, she left to take a similar position at Ohio State University, transitioning into the 2020 to 2021 academic year. Jim Malatras was appointed as Chancellor of the SUNY 64-campus system in late-August of 2020. As of fall of 2020, SUNY's enrollment was just under 400,000 students, so, a large number of people were to be affected by any policies implemented. Prior to his forced resignation in December 2021 due to a political crisis that was unrelated to his SUNY role, Malatras's response to the COVID crisis was generally regarded very highly. Malatras quickly called for measures to ensure the general safety of students' and employees' health, even encouraging the development of testing tools by the system's medical colleges.

While some policies responding to the pandemic had been in place at the end of the previous academic year (May/June), many colleges and universities struggled to develop plans for the new academic year; masking had been widely used and a vaccination for the virus had been developed and made public. Further, many restrictions related to the pandemic's early stages had been loosened by August because of the pandemic's perceived decline. There were still cases, and another surge during the fall was predicted by many health experts as many people moved to more indoor activities. However, colleges and universities had to develop their own policies to manage delivery of courses and keeping students and employees safe from the pandemic's spread.

Only a couple of weeks after his appointment, Malatras announced a formal "3-pronged approach" to addressing the pandemic. The approach integrated: "increased and quicker pooled tests, stricter enforcement of rules governing student behavior, and a new statewide SUNY dashboard that will display prompt and comprehensive statistics from each campus."[1] The announcement was made at the Jacobs School of Medicine and Biomedical Sciences, which is part of the campus's medical college. Dellacontrada, also, notes that at that media session, Malatras called attention to the leadership of the campus presidents throughout the SUNY system and how they were supervising implementation of policies on their own campuses. He quoted Malatras: "'The great presidents of the Western New York region are true leaders,' Malatras said. 'They have put forth robust plans to bring our students back safely and to instill confidence that we are doing things right…that we can remain open and safely.'"[2]

Finally, in late September, Malatras issued a policy statement to all SUNY campus presidents acknowledging strict penalties on violations of COVID-related health safety protocols. The 7-page letter enumerates 12 types of violations and related penalties, while also noting rights to due process and consideration of intentionality of the violation.[3]

In late 2020, as students were planning for a Thanksgiving break, Malatras implemented a testing requirement on students as well. The policy applied to all SUNY students who had been using on-campus facilities. These students had to test negative for COVID-19 before they would have left for the Thanksgiving break, and delivery of instruction after that break would be entirely remote.

In early February 2021, as the Spring semester began, Malatras announced the construction of a new medical facility in Buffalo's campus that would be able to process large amounts of COVID tests. According to Geddes,

> Chancellor Malatras recently increased testing frequency of all students, faculty, and staff on campus to at least once a week and the new Upstate Medical and partner Quadrant Biosciences lab at UB will be able to process 150,000 tests a week, increasing the total testing 350,000 tests per week across SUNY, with results being returned to campuses within 24 hours.[4]

Geddes noted that the lab would be operational by March 1 as well. In addition to the new facility, in September 2021, Malatras was able to announce a new testing protocol that had been developed by researchers within the SUNY's medical college system in collaboration with private entities. Geddes quoted Malatras as stating,

> Today's New York State Department of Health's approval of SUNY Upstate's research and testing technology is a game-changer for our 64 colleges and universities, because it is cost-effective for our campuses and less invasive for our students," said Chancellor Malatras. "Testing is one part of New York State's multipronged strategy to fight off a resurgence of the coronavirus pandemic. Today's approval shows that SUNY has all the intellectual and operational firepower to help tame the COVID beast. My thanks to Governor Cuomo, the New York State Department of Health SUNY Upstate's team of nation-leading faculty and researchers, and our public and private partners for this significant breakthrough."[5]

The procedure probably was in the works prior to Malatras's appointment, but he was able to make the announcement about the collaboration and in-house development of the protocol and test and its approval.

Consider how Malatras's statements and where he made the statements make a certain impact on audiences.

Case Questions

1. Identify ways that the speaker tries to mirror their audience in their words, narrative, or visually.
2. How might the audience be able to perceive mirroring with the speaker in their words, narrative, or visually (response to this may not be same as that for 1)?
3. Identify specific narratives used by the speaker and how members of the audience could relate to them.
4. Has the speaker conveyed trustworthiness? How/how not?
5. How could the speaker improve their message relative to engaging mirror neurons?
6. How could the speaker improve their message by engaging reward neurons?
7. How might another organization use this case as a narrative to facilitate change?

Artificial Intelligence/ChatGPT

The development of artificial intelligence tools has grown to a level at which it is now possible for such tools to create interactive experiences using chatbots instead of humans, draft entire documents—including graphics and facilitate research at speeds never before seen. Many companies have embraced these tools to improve efficiencies. One such company is Coca-Cola, which collaborated with a few tech companies with expertise in AI to create a commercial that aired on television during the Christmas Holiday Season in 2024, and the tools included ability for viewers to interact with Santa Claus in many different languages. These kinds of developments change marketing approaches but also require individual change in employees and customers.

AI tools threaten employees whose jobs may be performed by technology. As AI is introduced more aggressively into work, people and organizations are still learning how to use the new tools and how to balance human concerns with the desire for quality and efficiency.

DiPlacido notes several challenges creators faced with AI, which generated some backlash. While the campaign, which started in the 1990s, typically used real actors and integrated some graphics, the 2024 Coca-Cola commercial was entirely developed using AI tools. DiPlacido notes that several details are obviously inconsistent with reality. Among issues visible to viewers, he lists: trucks moving very quickly and seeming to glide, humans disproportionate to other features shown as well as buildings that seemed unrealistic in their shapes. So, even those experts at the tech companies involved could not yet figure out how to manipulate the product to avoid these design issues.[6]

DiPlacido goes on to indicate that many who work in marketing were unimpressed generally, concerned that the commercial showed that the shift to AI would compromise quality. Citing social media posts from a handful of marketers, he calls attention to the comments that humans are still able to develop the most realistic images to use in commercials.[7]

Coca-Cola is also using AI to facilitate "chats" with Santa Claus. Chatbots have been around for some time; they take the form of a popup to facilitate communication as if talking with someone via the computer keyboard. Such bots are able to generate responses to common questions and concerns customers might have about an experience or product. Coca-Cola is using ChatGPT as such a tool to create an entertaining experience as part of its public relations. It is able to respond to users' questions as if talking to a real person. Because chatbots have been used for some time, it may be possible for users to adapt to it much more quickly than to newer, less known tools.

At the same time, however, such chatbots need to be adequately trained by those who program them. As was seen with the issues affecting the Santa commercial, the technology is still evolving.

Discussion

1. What experience do you have with chatbots? If you have interacted with a chatbot or experienced AI in the workplace or school setting, describe how you used it as if sharing the experience with a friend or co-worker who has not used it.

2. How does your description of your experience help you or others understand how to use such tools if one has not used them before?
3. How can companies use Coca-Cola's "narrative" to improve their own use of AI while balancing human employees' needs?

Conclusion

Let's refer back to Figure 3.1, the rubric we used to guide development and assessment of narratives related to risk, crises, and change in technical contexts.

The rubric attempts to capture a large portion of the influences in the effectiveness of such narratives. Some of the cases in this book have included consideration of more of the factors than have others. Intentionally, I have limited the scope of consideration of narratives related to risk, crisis, and change within technical and scientific contexts so that I could more easily manage case inclusion and analyses. However, the rubric has some admitted limitations.

There are many ways to approach analysis of framing of risk, crisis, and change communication in technical settings. For example, while we considered various factors that influence trust in the source of the narrative and related mirroring dynamics, we did not consider issues related to the race, gender, culture, or physical and medical conditions of the source that may impact trust and mirroring. Also as noted much earlier in this book, there is a body of scholarship about the use of metaphorical or fictional narratives. The proposed framework avoids such narratives, because they are considered weaker forms of narrative.

Beyond these considerations, counternarratives—narratives that are part of a counterargument related to a discussion about a proposed change, for example—can be considered as well. Another rhetorical concept, *Kairos*—or timeliness/appropriateness of timing of a message—may be considered further. At what time upon recognizing a risk or crisis is it appropriate to communicate actions to address it? Developing an effective message may take some time; however, ethical considerations generally require communication about risk or crises as soon as possible.

Elements like the ones discussed in this concluding section also raise the point of ethical development and use of narratives. A fictional narrative describes something that did not happen or likely could not happen, and it represents the event as if it could happen. While frequently found in literature and film, how do fictional narratives function within technical communication settings involving risks, crises, and change? If a reader/audience in such a context believes such a narrative to be true and acts on the information to be safe from risk or crisis, the particular narrative may be considered effective. If it is not acknowledged to be fictional, is it ethical to use it? Also, relative to *Kairos*, or appropriate timing, is it ethical to delay or even withhold information about risks or crises? There is the example of the space shuttle Columbia disaster in 2003, of which it has been reported that the crew was never informed of the damage the space shuttle experienced at launch and the risk that the damage posed for them upon re-entry.[1,2]

During blast-off, a piece of the orbiter's fuel tank came off and hit the shuttle, damaging its thermal insulation—important for absorbing and shielding the interior of the shuttle from the heat generated during re-entry. Having analyzed its options during the mission, NASA engineers were aware of the risks such damage posed, but they had no way of repairing it or getting another spacecraft up to retrieve the crew. The ground team decided not to inform the crew of the damage and risk, since there was nothing that anyone could do about it. If you were one of the astronauts in that situation, would you want to know that you could possibly die during re-entry?

Finally, as noted with a few of the cases related to the COVID-pandemic policies, cryptocurrency investing, and EV development, the political environment can affect perception of risks and related narratives: the degree to which government regulations are involved or a given policy may enable or restrict behaviors to address risks. Again, during the COVID pandemic, there was much debate about balancing mask and vaccine mandates with personal liberties in addressing the personal risks and the crisis facing hospitals. The lack of regulations and a formal asset by which to back cryptocurrencies contributed to the risks of such investments and crises related to crashes of a few such currencies.

Again, many of these elements and approaches to analysis and critique have been discussed in other works; however, more might be done to develop a framework that includes such elements in addition to the framework presented in this book.

Additional Cases for Practice

Information Technology Security Hacking.

As electronic information technologies have grown, more businesses, financial institutions, and the general public have increasingly felt more comfortable conducting business and related purchases online using credit cards and other private financial tools. From the earliest stages of "e-business" or "e-commerce," there was concern about the security of these information systems and related networks. People and businesses were giving personal information to entities that facilitated transactions, including credit and financial accounts access, via electronic information systems. Depending on security systems in place, these systems might expose thousands to millions of people to financial fraud. Even as security systems evolve, we frequently hear of systems being "hacked" or breached. Obviously, there are risks inherent in doing business online; and sometimes a crisis occurs when a large company's financial information system is "hacked." However, these risks are not limited to financial information. Healthcare systems are being hacked as well, exposing patients' medical records as well as financial information to fraud.

Many websites and texts exist that address strategies and tactics to minimize hacking threats for businesses, and much training goes into how IT staff can monitor such threats. However, fewer resources exist on how to respond to such hacks. How an organization responds to such hacks is important, because so many people can feel helpless and can lose large sums of money to such hacks.

The three cases presented here provide layered analysis practice related to these risks and crises that may require changes within systems. The first case pertains to a healthcare system hack resulting in theft, the second pertains to a large financial system hack affecting over 100 million people, and the last pertains to a personal experience related to a smaller-scale financial system hack. As with chapter-specific exercises, each case here includes several questions to encourage practice and application of concepts provided in the book. With each case, in addition to the discussion questions posed, consider how another organization might use the case as a narrative to facilitate change.

Healthcare Hack

Kolbasuk-McGee[1] reported that as of late February 2022, "64 reported health data breaches, affecting a total of nearly 3.1 million individuals" had been reported to a government website that tracks such breaches. Kolbasuk-McGee further acknowledged that of these, "nearly 80 percent of the breaches posted on the HHS OCR website in 2022 were reported as hacking/IT incidents, and those incidents were responsible for 96 percent of individuals affected so far this year by major health data breaches." Some of these are ransomware attacks; basically, the hacker(s) access personal data of customers/patients and then demand some fee not to release the data. Most often, this information includes name and social security number as well as any billing information or financial accounts on file. One such incident actually involved the theft of a backup server for a hospital system.

Among the largest hacks affecting healthcare providers, Kolbasuk-McGee included, a "hacking incident involving data exfiltration, affecting 1.3 million individuals, reported on Jan. 2 by Florida-based North Broward Hospital District, which does business as Broward Health."[2] The incident actually occurred in late 2021 and involved a stolen backup imaging server that contained sensitive information, including "patients' names, social security numbers, health insurance information, radiology imaging, and/or other related medical information."[3] South City Hospital issued a 12-page release acknowledging the breach, what it entailed, and what action patients could take. Perhaps the most vital information shared in the document was what action the hospital system was taking.

In the section describing action the hospital system took, they state that actions included: "reviewing existing security policies to further protect against similar incidents moving forward. We are notifying potentially impacted individuals, so that they may take steps to best protect their information, should they feel it is appropriate to do so."[4] Further, they acknowledge that affected patients will receive a letter with specific details, and they provide a phone number patients can use to contact them with any questions.

In the section detailing "What you can do," they state, "South City Hospital encourages you to remain vigilant against incidents of identity theft and fraud, to review your account statements, and to monitor your credit reports for suspicious activity. Under U.S. law, you are entitled to one free credit report annually from each of the three major credit reporting bureaus."[5] They, also, encourage implementing a credit freeze and show how to do that. They, then, provide phone numbers and other contact information for the major credit reporting agencies as well as state agencies that may help.

Questions

1. Beyond the 12-page document and letter to affected patients, what other media could have been used to communicate with patients?
2. Professional narratives are included: where are they?
3. How could personal narratives have been integrated/used?
4. What impact might personal narratives have had on affected patients?
5. How does the hospital system try to establish trustworthiness in the document?
6. As you view the entire document, do you think that patients feel a sense of trust in the hospital's systems?
7. Other than the usual statement about reviewing its security measures, what other possible changes in its operations or systems could the system implement to reassure patients and the public, and how could it best communicate those considerations and changes?
8. Can patients do anything to avoid such risks, beyond what the hospital offered?

Capital One Bank Hack

In July 2019, Capital One Bank's IT system was breached by an individual. Based on their own estimates, Capital One reported that, "this event affected approximately 100 million individuals in the United States and approximately 6 million in Canada."[6] In September 2019, Capital One announced that the person who hacked their system had been caught by the FBI and indicated that there is "no evidence the data was used for fraud or shared by this individual."[7] Further, Capital One acknowledged that the affected data included credit scores, credit limits, balances, payment history, contact information, some transaction data, social security numbers of credit card customers, and bank account numbers of secured credit card customers.

Included in Capital One's September 2019 message is a statement from its CEO: "While I am grateful that the perpetrator has been caught, I am deeply sorry for what has happened. I sincerely apologize for the understandable worry this incident must be causing those affected and I am committed to making it right." Indeed, Capital One reached a settlement related to this incident and made an effort to allay fears of customers while trying to regain their trust. In the settlement, customers were able to use any of several avenues to be compensated if they were directly affected, and Capital One would be proactive in helping to monitor their credit reports.[8] The settlement site provides further information about customers' legal rights and how to submit claims.[9]

Questions

1. Beyond the websites that are updated periodically, what other media could have been used to communicate with customers?
2. Professional narratives are included: where are they?
3. Are any personal narratives included? If so, where?
4. How could personal narratives have been better integrated/used?
5. What impact might personal narratives have had on affected customers?
6. How does the financial institution try to establish trustworthiness in their websites?
7. In you view the websites, do you think that customers feel a sense of trust in the company? Why/why not?
8. Other than the usual statement about reviewing its security measures, what other possible changes in its operations or systems could the financial institution implement to reassure customers and the public, and how could it communicate those considerations and changes?

9. Beyond what the bank provided, can customers change anything about the way they apply for credit cards to address such risks and crises?

Professional Organization's Financial Hack

As many professionals do, I have memberships in multiple professional organizations. Many of these organizations use electronic means, including third-party vendors, to process membership fees and conference registration fees. Consequently, this data is susceptible to being hacked. While these instances get much less coverage in the news, they can still affect both the organization and its members. Shortly after renewing my membership in one such organization, I received a message from the organization's communication team alerting me (and others) about a security breach. The organization uses a third-party vendor for such transactions, and the vendor had let the organization know about the breach.

In the email message that acknowledged the breach, the communication team states, "It is therefore possible that an unknown individual may have used the code to capture credit card form information during the registration process." They also state that the vendor removed the irregular code and implemented additional measures to secure its system.

Also in the message, the organization acknowledges that the organization, "has two members who have reported similar unauthorized charges after purchasing their memberships. Please take any steps that you deem necessary to protect your security. We recommend that you review your credit card statement. If you see anything suspicious, please notify your credit card issuer and ask for a replacement card." The message goes on to identify ways to monitor credit card activity for fraud and how to report any fraud.

A few months after I received this message, I noticed unfamiliar charges on my credit card statement. I immediately called the credit card vendor and reported the activity. They closed my account and issued me a new card. I also used the reporting system provided with the message to report the activity to the organization who would then send to the vendor.

Questions

1. Beyond the email message, what other media could have been used to communicate with members?
2. Professional narratives are included: where are they?
3. Are any personal narratives included? If so, where?
4. How could personal narratives have been better integrated/used?
5. What impact could personal narratives have on affected members?
6. How do the organization and vendor try to establish trustworthiness in the email message?
7. Would you feel a sense of trust in the organization or vendor? Why/why not?
8. Other than the usual statement about reviewing its security measures, what possible changes in its operations or systems could the organization or vendor implement to reassure members, and how could it communicate those considerations and changes?
9. What changes could I make to my payment practices as a customer/member?

Layoffs at Technical Firms

The two cases that follow pertain to the technology impact that the economic downturn during and shortly after the COVID pandemic had on companies. While layoffs themselves may not be directly related to technical issues, as noted earlier, they can involve complex systems that include specialized entities and expertise. How an organization manages the process of laying off employees becomes its own narrative that other organizations may use in assessing how to manage their own such situations.

Amazon

In late 2022, Amazon began laying off some employees. Thorbecke reported that, according to an Amazon spokesperson, "…given the current macro-economic environment (as well as several years of rapid hiring), some teams are making adjustments, which in some cases means certain roles are no longer necessary."[10] Further, according to Thorbecke, "after reaching record highs during the pandemic, shares of Amazon have shed more than 40 percent in 2022 so far."[11] So, many of the decisions to lay off employees were related to investor reactions to the effects of the macroeconomy that impact earnings reports. Nevertheless, employees needed to be notified of layoffs.

The Amazon spokesperson also indicated that the company was making an effort to help affected employees.[12] As layoffs continued into 2023, a memo that Amazon's CEO shared with employees was published. In it, he acknowledges reasons for the layoffs and which sectors of the business would be affected by the current round. He explains why the announcement of the new round of layoffs is separate from the previous round:

> Some may ask why we didn't announce these role reductions with the ones we announced a couple months ago. The short answer is that not all of the teams were done with their analyses in the late fall; and rather than rush through these assessments without the appropriate diligence, we chose to share these decisions as we've made them so people had the information as soon as possible. The same is true for this note as the impacted teams are not yet finished making final decisions on precisely which roles will be impacted.
>
> …To those ultimately impacted by these reductions, I want to thank you for the work you have done on behalf of customers and the company. It's never easy to say goodbye to our teammates, and you will be missed.[13]

As layoffs continued into 2025, Shibu reports that the company continues to state its support for affected employees. However, publicly, the company continues to explain reasons for continued layoffs by noting financial and stock performance related reasons. Further, as many companies have done post-pandemic, Amazon has stepped up "return-to-office" efforts. Shibu noted that some employees perceived this to be a "backdoor layoff," as reports circulate about tech companies using RTO mandates to lay off any employees who refuse.[14]

Discussion

Access the articles and messages from Amazon's leadership regarding lay-offs that are available online.

Questions

1. How would you assess emotional intelligence as represented in these messages relative to investors? Relative to employees?
2. How has the company demonstrated consideration for each audience?
3. How could leadership have announced actions more effectively?

Bristol Myers Squibb

An ongoing challenge for pharmaceutical companies is the impact of ex-piring patents. As patents expire, the company loses revenue as more com-petition is introduced through generic medications produced by other companies. When combined with a general downturn in the economy, this impact is harder to address. In 2024, Bristol Myers Squibb began laying off employees as part of a restructuring effort. The move affected about 6 percent of its workforce while the announcement included ac-knowledgment of the effort to improve growth and earnings.[15] Again, these reasons appeal to investors/shareholders, the impact on employees must also be addressed.

In 2025, Kansteiner reported another round of layoffs, affecting a smaller number of employees. As is typical in such announcements industry-wide, Kansteiner acknowledged that a spokesperson stated, "'Unfortunately, there have been impacts to some of our employees as a result of these changes'; she continued, adding that the company is 'grateful for the contributions of our colleagues and a top priority for us is supporting employees throughout the transition process.'"[16]

Discussion

Access any articles and messages available online related to the Bristol Myers Squibb series of layoffs.

Questions

1. How would you assess emotional intelligence as represented in the messages relative to investors? Relative to employees?
2. How has the company demonstrated consideration for each audience?
3. How could leadership have announced actions more effectively?
4. How can companies do more in public announcements to convey support for employees?

Notes

Chapter 1

1. Angeli (2023, 75–6).
2. Scott (2023, 257).
3. Flynn (2015).
4. Hoff-Clausen (2013).
5. Offerdal, et al. (2021).
6. Scott (2023, 254).
7. Remley (2019).
8. Remley (2015).
9. Remley (2017b).
10. Remley (2017a).
11. Remley (2019).
12. Grabill and Simmons (1998).
13. Caruso and Salovey (2004, 9–21).
14. Pillay (2011).
15. Bradberry and Greaves (2009).
16. Bradberry and Greaves (2009).
17. Remley (2019).
18. Remley (2017a).
19. Remley (2019).
20. Millar and Backer-Beck (2004).
21. Millar and Backer-Beck (2004).
22. Zak (2014).
23. Zak (2017).
24. Hagle (2022).

Chapter 2

1. Remley (2017a and b).
2. Aristotle (1991).
3. Simons and Jones (2011, 124).
4. Calvert et al. (2004, xii).
5. Aristotle (1991).
6. Perelman and Olbrechts-Tyteca (1969, 25).

7. Perelman and Olbrechts-Tyteca (1969, 25).
8. Perelman and Olbrechts-Tyteca (1969).
9. Perelman and Olbrechts-Tyteca (1969).
10. New London Group (1996).
11. Sheridan et al. (2012, xiv).
12. Remley (2017a and b).
13. Bethge et al. (2003).
14. Bremner and Spence (2008).
15. Moreno and Mayer (2000).
16. Malecki et al. (2021).

Chapter 3

1. Flynn (2015).
2. Dahlstrom (2014).
3. Marty and McDermott (1985).
4. Marty and McDermott (1986).
5. Rook (1987).
6. Larkey and Gonzalez (2007).
7. Kim et al. (2012).
8. Cox and Cox (2001).
9. Hillenbrand and Verrina (2022).
10. Murphy-Hoefer et al. (2020).
11. Ricketts (2007).
12. Gallo (2018).
13. Denning (2008).
14. Saltmarshe (2018).
15. Zak (2015).
16. Flynn (2015).
17. Heidari-Robinson and Heywood (2016).

Chapter 4

1. Examples.com (2025).
2. Ray et al. (2025).
3. Levinson (2012).
4. Menon and Rainer (2022, 9).
5. Menon and Rainer (2022, 9).
6. Peregrine (2024).
7. NBAA (2025).

8. NTSB (2022).
9. NTSB (2009, 10).
10. NTSB (2010, 67).

Chapter 5

1. Schmalzle et al. (2013).
2. Golding et al. (1992).
3. Malecki et al. (2021).
4. Bob (2021).
5. Bob (2021).
6. Ohio Department of Health (2020).

Risk Communication Case Activities

1. Eddy (2022).
2. Eddy (2022).
3. France-Presse (2022).
4. Hurd (2022).
5. Yahoo Finance (2022).
6. Shnurenko (2018).
7. Bybit.com (2021).
8. Bybit.com (2021).

Chapter 6

1. Heath and Millar (2004, 4).
2. Heath and Millar (2004, 12).
3. Heath and Millar (2004, 13).
4. Caruso and Salovey (2004, 25).
5. Bradberry and Greaves (2009, 191).
6. Bradberry and Greaves (2009, 179).
7. Zak (2015).
8. Remley (2019).
9. Malecki et al. (2021).
10. Fiske, Cuddy, and Glick (2007).
11. Gallo (2018).
12. Saltmarshe (2018).
13. Flynn (2015).
14. Remley (2019).

15. Coatney (2020).
16. Golding et al. (1992).
17. Dahlstrom (2014).
18. Hagle (2022).

Crisis Communication Case Activities

1. Sandor and Genç (2022).
2. Cyrus.ismoney.eth (2022).
3. Sandor and Genç (2022).
4. Ammara (2022).
5. Dey (2022).
6. Chaturvedi (2022).
7. Mourya (2022).
8. Brown (2022).
9. Scholartrix (2022).
10. Quiroz-Gutierrez (2022).
11. Deliso (2024).
12. Pendleton (2023).

Chapter 7

1. Krisher (2021).
2. Krisher (2021).
3. Hawkins (2021).
4. Hawkins (2021).
5. LaReau (2021).
6. LaReau (2021).
7. Garsten (2022).
8. Haas (1999).
9. Norman (2013).
10. Division of Information Technology, Kent State University and Kent State Online (2022, 4).
11. Fenson (2000, para. 7).
12. Rayzer (2021).

Change Communication Case Activities

1. SUNY Chancellor Announces three-Pronged Attack on Campus Covid (2020).
2. Dellacontrada (2020).

3. Malatras (2020).
4. Geddes (2021a).
5. Geddes (2021b).
6. DiPlacido (2024).
7. DiPlacido (2024).

Conclusion

1. ABC News (2013).
2. CBC (2013).

Additional Cases for Practices

1. Kolbasuk-McGee (2022).
2. Kolbasuk-McGee (2022).
3. Onetrustdataguidance.com (2022)
4. South City Hospital (2022, 4).
5. South City Hospital (2022, 5).
6. Capital One (2022a).
7. Capital One (2022a).
8. Capital One (2022b).
9. Capital One (2022b).
10. Thorbecke (2022).
11. Thorbecke (2022).
12. Thorbecke (2022)
13. Palmer (2023).
14. Shibu (2025).
15. Pagliarulo (2024).
16. Kansteiner (2025).

References

ABC News. 2013. "Columbia Shuttle Crew Not Told of Possible Problem With Reentry." https://abcnews.go.com/Technology/columbia-shuttle-crew-told-problem-reentry/story?id=18366185.

Agence France-Presse. 2022. "Mercedes-Benz Issues Global Recall of One Million Older Cars." *The Guardian*, June 4. https://www.theguardian.com/technology/2022/jun/04/mercedes-benz-issues-global-recalls-of-one-million-older-cars.

Ammara. 2022. "Why Terra Founder Is Not Speaking About LUNC—Has Do Kwon Abandoned Luna Classic (LUNC)?" *The Crypto Basic*, June 2. https://thecryptobasic.com/2022/06/06/why-terra-founder-is-not-speaking-about-lunc-has-do-kwon-abandoned-luna-classic-lunc/.

Angeli, Elizabeth L. 2023. "Crisis Communication." In *Keywords in Technical and Professional Communication*, edited by Han Yu and Jonathan Beuhl. UP of Colorado.

Aristotle. 1991. *The Art of Rhetoric*. Translated by H.C. Lawson-Tancred. Penguin.

Bethge, Matthias., David Rotermund, and Klaus R. Pawelzik. 2003. "Optimal Neural Rate Coding Leads to Bimodal Firing Rate Distributions." *Network Computation in Neural Systems* 14 (2): 303–19.

Bob, M. 2021. "2020 Ford Escape: Recalls Worth Knowing About." *Vehicle History*, March 6.

Bradberry, Travis, and Jean Greaves. 2009. *Emotional Intelligence 2.0*. TalentSmart.

Bremner, Andrew J., and C. Spence. 2008. "Unimodal Experience Constrains While Multisensory Experiences Enrich Cognitive Construction." *Behavioral and Brain Sciences* 31: 335–6.

Brown, Albert. 2022. "Terra Founder Do Kwon Says He Never Sold UST Nor LUNA During Price Crash." *The Crypto Basic*, May 14. https://thecryptobasic.com/2022/05/14/terra-founder-do-kwon-says-he-never-sold-ust-nor-luna-during-price-crash/.

Bybit.com. 2021. "What Are the Risks of Cryptocurrencies?" *Bybit/Learn*, March 18. https://learn.bybit.com/crypto/what-are-the-risks-of-cryptocurrencies/.

Calvert, Gemma, A, Charles Spence and Barry E. Stein (eds). 2004. The Handbook of Multisensory Processes. The MIT Press.

Capital One. 2022a. "Information on the Capital One Cyber Incident." April 22. https://www.capitalone.com/digital/facts2019/.

Capital One. 2022b. "Capital One Data Breach Class Action Settlement." https://www.capitalonesettlement.com/en.

Caruso, David, and Peter Salovey. 2004. *The Emotionally Intelligent Manager.* Jossey-Bass.

CBC. 2013. "NASA Discussed Not Telling Astronauts About Columbia's Doom. NASA Discussed Not Telling Astronauts About Columbia's Doom." https://www.cbc.ca/news/science/nasa-discussed-not-telling-astronauts-about-columbia-s-doom-1.1390174.

Chaturvedi, Aakanksha. 2022. "Terra Luna Crashes 97%: Was Do Kwon Responsible for Another Failed Stablecoin?" *Business Today,* May 12. https://www.businesstoday.in/crypto/story/terra-luna-crashes-97-was-do-kwon-responsible-for-another-failed-stablecoin-333265-2022-05-12.

Coatney, Caryn. 2020. "Communicating Compassionately in a Crisis: John Curtin and Journalists, 1941–1945." *International Journal of Humanities and Social Science* 10 (12): 36–45.

Cox, Dena, and Anthony D. Cox. 2001. "Communicating the Consequences of Early Detection: The Role of Evidence and Framing." *Journal of Marketing* 65: 91–103.

Cyrus.ismoney.eth. 2022. "Twitter Posting." https://twitter.com/cyounessi1/status/1524910207838699520.

Dahlstrom, Michael F. 2014. "Using Narratives and Storytelling to Communicate Science with Nonexpert Audiences." *Proceedings of the National Academy of Sciences of the United States of America* 111 (Suppl 4): 13614–20. https://doi.org/10.1073/pnas.1320645111.

Deliso, Meredith. 2024. "East Palestine Derailment: Timeline of Key Events in Toxic Train Disaster." ABCNews.com. https://abcnews.go.com/US/east-palestine-derailment-timeline-key-events-toxic-train/story?id=97522161.

Dellacontrada, John. 2020. "SUNY Chancellor Touts New COVID-19 Measures in Visit to UB." *University at Buffalo,* September 8. https://www.buffalo.edu/ubnow/stories/2020/09/chancellor-visit.html.

Denning, Steve. 2008. "How Leaders Can Use Powerful Narratives as Change Catalysts." *Strategy & Leadership* 36 (2): 11–15. https://doi.org/10.1108/10878570810857528.

Dey, Kunal. 2022. "Who is Do Kwon? TerraUSD Founder Alleged to be Behind Crypto Bloodbath." *Media Entertainment Arts WorldWide,* May 13. https://meaww.com/do-kwon-terra-usd-founder-crypto.

DiPlacido, Dan. 2024. "Coca Cola's AI-Generated Ad Controversy, Explained." *Forbes.* https://www.forbes.com/sites/danidiplacido/2024/11/16/coca-colas-ai-generated-ad-controversy-explained/.

Division of Information Technology, Kent State University, and Kent State Online. 2022 *Canvas Blackboard Comparison: Instructor Guidebook.*

Eddy, Melissa. 2022. "Mercedes-Benz Recalls Nearly 1 Million Vehicles Over Brake Issue." *New York Times*, June 6. https://www.nytimes.com/2022/06/06 /business/mercedes-benz-brake-recall.html.

Fenson, Sarah. 2000. "10 Tips for Communicating Change." *Inc*, June 1. https:// www.inc.com/articles/2000/06/19312.html. Accessed February 20, 2018.

Fiske, Susan T., Amy J. C. Cuddy and Peter Glick. 2007. Universal dimensions of social cognition: Warmth and competence. *Trends in Cognitive Sciences* 11 (2): 77–83.

Flynn, Terry. 2015. "How Narratives Can Reduce Resistance and Change Attitudes: Insights from Behavioral Science can Enhance Public Relations Research and Practice." *Research Journal of the Institute for Public Relations* 2: 2 (October, 2015). Flynn.RJManuscript.8Nov2015-FORMATTED.pdf.

Gallo, Carmine. 2018. "Jeff Bezos Banned PowerPoint in Meetings. His Replacement Is Brilliant. Narrative Memos Have Replaced PowerPoint Presentations at Amazon. Here Are 3 Reasons." *INC*, April 2018. https://www.inc.com /carmine-gallo/jeff-bezos-bans-powerpoint-in-meetings-his-replacement-is -brilliant.html.

Garsten, Ed. 2022. "Mary Barra Makes GM's Electric Future Clearer as Company Reports 2021 Profit." *Forbes*, February 1. https://www.forbes.com/sites /edgarsten/2022/02/01/mary-barra-makes-gms-electric-future-clearer-as -company-reports-2021-profit/?sh=6bff1e004f3a.

Geddes, Daryl. 2021a. "Chancellor Malatras Announces SUNY Upstate Medical University to Construct a COVID-19 Testing Laboratory at the University at Buffalo to Increase Capacity and Speed Up Analysis as SUNY Campuses Reopen." *Upstate News*, February 1. https://www.upstate.edu/news/articles /2021/2021-02-01-chancbuff.php.

Geddes, Daryl, 2021b. "SUNY Chancellor Malatras and Upstate Medical Interim President Dewan Announce State Health Department Approval of Upstate's Saliva Diagnostic Test to Quickly Identify Positive COVID Cases." *Upstate News*, September 1. https://www.upstate.edu/news/articles /2020/2020-09-01-chancellorcovid.php.

Golding, Dominic, Sheldon Krimsky, and Alonzo Plough. 1992. "Evaluating Risk Communication: Narrative vs. Technical Presentations of Information about Radon." *Risk Analysis* 12: 27–35. https://doi.org/10.1111/j.1539-6924.1992. tb01304.x.

Grabill, Jeffrey T., and W. Michele Simmons. 1998. "Toward a Critical Rhetoric of Risk Communication: Producing Citizens and the Role of Technical Communicators." *Technical Communication Quarterly* 7 (4): 415–41. https://doi .org/10.1080/10572259809364640.

Hagle, John. 2022. "How Inspiring Narratives Can Help Restore and Build Trust." *World Economic Forum*. https://www.weforum.org/agenda/2022/02 /narratives-trust-fear-opportunities/.

Haas, Christina. 1999. "On the Relationship Between Old and New Technologies." *Computers and Composition* 16: 209–28. https://doi.org/10.1016 /S8755-4615(99)00003-1.

Hawkins, Andrew J. 2021. "GM Unveils New Logo to Emphasize Its Pivot to Electric Vehicles." *The Verge*, January 8. https://www.theverge .com/2021/1/8/22220574/gm-new-logo-electric-vehicle-brand-ces-2021.

Heath, Robert. L., and Dan P. Millar. 2004. "A Rhetorical Approach to Crisis Communication; Management, Communication Processes, and Strategic Responses." In *Responding to Crisis: A Rhetorical Approach to Crisis Communication*, edited by Dan P. Millar and Robert L. Heath. Lawrence Erlbaum Associates, Inc.

Heidari-Robinson, Stephen, and Suzanne Heywood. 2016. "Opinion: Why Company Reorganizations Fail and How to Make Them Work." *Marketwatch.com*, November 15. https://www.marketwatch.com/story/how-companies-can-reorganize -to-make-investors-money-2016-11-15.

Hillenbrand, Adrian, and Eugenio Verrina. 2022. "The Asymmetric Effect of Narratives on Prosocial Behavior." *Games and Economic Behavior* 135: 241–70. https://doi.org/10.1016/j.geb.2022.06.008.

Hoff-Clausen, Elisabeth. 2013. "Attributing Rhetorical Agency in a Crisis of Trust: Danske Bank's Act of Public Listening after the Credit Collapse." *Rhetoric Society Quarterly* 43. https://doi.org/10.1080/02773945.2013 .839820.

Hurd, Byron. 2022. "Mercedes 'Do Not Drive' Brake Recall Expands to 1 Million Vehicles." *Autoblog*, June 6. https://www.autoblog.com/carbuying /mercedes-1million-vehicle-recall.

Examples.com. 2025. "Incident Report for Medication Error Example [Edit & Download]." https://www.examples.com/docs/incident-report-for-medication -error.html.

Kansteiner, Fraiser. 2025. "UPDATE: Bristol Myers' Cost-Savings Drive Claims Another 280 Jobs in US." *Fierce Pharma*. https://www.fiercepharma.com/pharma /bristol-myers-billion-dollar-cost-savings-drive-claims-another-223-jobs-nj.

Kim, Hyun Suk, Cabral A. Bigman, Amy E. Leader, Caryn Lerman, and Joseph N. Cappella. 2012. "Narrative Health Communication and Behavior Change: The Influence of Exemplars in the News on Intention to Quit Smoking." *Journal of Communication* 62 (3): 473–92. https://doi .org/10.1111/j.1460-2466.2012.01644.x.

Kolbasuk-McGee, Marianne. 2022. "Hacks Causing Most Big Health Data Breaches So Far in 2022." *GovInfoSecurity*, February 22. https://www.govinfosecurity .com/hacks-causing-most-big-health-data-breaches-so-far-in-2022-a-18586.

Krisher, Tom. 2021. "GM CEO Says Making Ventilators Changed the Company Culture." *U.S. News*, December 9. https://www.usnews.com

/news/business/articles/2021-12-09/gm-ceo-says-making-ventillators-changed-the-company-culture.

LaReau, Jamie. 2021. "GM Promises to Leave No One Behind As It Moves to an All-Electric Future." *Detroit Free Press*, June 29. https://www.freep.com/story/money/cars/general-motors/2021/06/29/gm-promises-leave-no-one-behin.d-all-electric-future/7796996002/.

Larkey, Linda K., and Julie Gonzalez. 2007. "Storytelling for Promoting Colorectal Cancer Prevention and Early Detection among Latinos." *Patient Education and Counseling* 67: 272–8.

Levinson, Daniel R. 2012. *Hospital Incident Reporting Systems Do Not Capture Most Patient Harm*. Department of Health and Human Services.

Malatras, Jim. 2020. "Letter." *The State University of New York*. https://www.suny.edu/media/suny/content-assets/documents/chancellor/UniformSanctions-Response-COVID-19-Student-Violations.pdf.

Malecki, Kristen, Julie A. Keating, and Nasir Safdar. 2021. "Crisis Communication and Public Perception of COVID-19 Risk in the Era of Social Media." *Clinical Infectious Diseases* 72 (4): 697–702. https://doi.org/10.1093/cid/ciaa758.

Marty, Phillip. J., and Robert J. McDermott. 1985. "Effects of Two Testicular Cancer Education Programs on Self-examination Knowledge and Attitudes Among College-aged Men." *Health Education* 16: 33–6.

Marty, Phillip J., and Robert J. McDermott. 1986. "Three Strategies for Encouraging Testicular Self Examination Among College-Aged Males." *Journal of American College Health* 34: 253–8.

Menon, Catherine, and Austen Rainer. 2022. "Stories and Narratives in Safety Engineering." *Conference Proceedings of 30th Safety Critical Systems Symposium*. https://www.researchgate.net/publication/359085619_Stories_and_narratives_in_safety_engineering.

Millar, Dan P., and Debra Backer-Beck. 2004. "Metaphors of Crisis." In *Responding to Crisis: A Rhetorical Approach to Crisis Communication*, edited by Dan P. Millar and Robert L, Heath. Lawrence Erlbaum Associates, Inc.

Moreno, Roxana, and Richard E. Mayer. 2000. "A Learner-Centered Approach to Multimedia Explanations: Deriving Instructional Design Principles from Cognitive Theory." *Interactive Multimedia Electronic Journal of Computer-Enhanced Learning* 2.

Mourya, Ekta. 2022. "Do Kwon Reappears After Terra's LUNA Crashes from $64 to $0.50 in 72 hours." *FXStreet*, May 11. https://www.fxstreet.com/cryptocurrencies/news/do-kwon-reappears-after-terras-luna-crashes-from-64-to-1-in-72-hours-202205111410.

Murphy-Hoefer, Rebecca, Kevin C. Davis, Brian A. King, Diane Beistle, Robert Rodes, Corinne Graffunder. 2020. Association Between the Tips from Former Smokers Campaign and Smoking Cessation Among Adults, United

States, 2012–2018. *Preventing Chronic Diseases* 17: 200052. http://doi
.org/10.5888/pcd17.200052.

National Business Aviation Association. 2025. "Case Studies of Narrative
Safety Reporting Programs." https://nbaa.org/aircraft-operations/safety
/safety-data-collection-analysis-and-sharing/narrative-safety-reporting/case
-studies-narrative-safety-reporting-programs/.

National Transportation Safety Board. 2009. "Operations/Human Performance
Group Chairmen Interview summaries." Flight crew. DCA09MA026.
Washington D.C.

National Transportation Safety Board. 2010. "Loss of Thrust in Both Engines
After Encountering a Flock of Birds and Subsequent Ditching on the Hudson
River, US Airways Flight 1549, Airbus A320-214, N106US, Weehawken,
New Jersey, January 15, 2009." Aircraft Accident Report NTSB/AAR-10/03.
Washington, DC.

National Transportation Safety Board. 2022. "Aviation Investigation Final
Report." *Cessna 120.*

New London Group. 1996. "A Pedagogy of Multiliteracies: Designing Social
Futures." *Harvard Educational Review* 66: 60–92.

Norman, Donald. 2013. *The Design of Everyday Things.* Basic Books.

Offerdal, Truls S., Sine N. Just, and Oyvind Ihlen. 2021. "Public Ethos in the
Pandemic Rhetorical Situation: Strategies for Building Trust in Authorities'
Risk Communication." *Journal of International Risk and Crisis Communica-
tion Research* 4: 2. https://doi.org/10.30658/jicrcr.4.2.3.

Ohio Department of Health. 2020. "Governor DeWine, Health Director Update
COVID-19 Prevention and Preparedness Plan." Press Release.

Onetrustdataguidance.com. 2022. "USA: South City Hospital Notifies OCR of
Data Security Incident." OneTrust DataGuidance, January 26. https://www.
dataguidance.com/news/usa-south-city-hospital-notifies-ocr-data-security.

Pagliarulo, Ned. 2024. "Bristol Myers to Cut 6% of Workforce, Trim Drug
Pipeline." *BioPharma Dive.* https://www.biopharmadive.com/news/bristol
-myers-layoffs-restructuring-cost-savings/714254/#:~:text=Bristol%20
Myers%20Squibb%20will%20cut%206%25%20of%20its,affect%
20some%202%2C200%20employees%2C%20the%20company%20
said%20Thursday.

Palmer, Annie. 2023. "Amazon to Lay off 9,000 More Workers in Addition to
Earlier Cuts." *CNBC.* https://www.cnbc.com/2023/03/20/amazon-layoffs
-company-to-cut-off-9000-more-workers.html?msockid=00a2a26f1
75060f03b4ab69616b76173

Pendleton, Pen. 2023. "Norfolk Southern Fumbles Its Crisis Response."
*O'Dwyers: The Inside News of Public Relations and Marketing Communica-
tions,* March 1. https://www.odwyerpr.com/story/public/19250/2023-03-01
/norfolk-southern-fumbles-its-crisis-response.html.

Peregrine, Zoey. 2024. "Improving Airline Safety Through Passenger Feedback Loops." *Wowfare.com.* https://wowfare.com/blog/improving-airline-safety -through-passenger-feedback-loops/.

Perelman, Chaim, and Lucie Olbrechts-Tyteca. 1969. *The New Rhetoric: A Treatise on Argumentation.* University of Notre Dame Press.

Pillay, Srinivasan S. 2011. *Your Brain and Business.* Pearson/Financial Times.

Quiroz-Gutierrez, Marco. 2022. "The New Crypto Bill Could End Algorithmic Stablecoins as We Know Them." *Fortune Crypto*, June 8. https://fortune .com/crypto/2022/06/08/algorithmic-stablecoins-terra-luna-crypto-regula- tion-senate-bill-lummis-gillibrand/.

Ray, Unmessa, Cristian Arteaga, Inwha Oh, and Jeenwoong Park. 2025. "Unveiling Untapped Potential: Leveraging Accident Narratives for Enhanced Construction Safety Management." *Journal of Management in Engineering* 41: 3. https://doi.org/10.1061/JMENEA.MEENG-6397.

Rayzer, Alexus. 2021. "From Blackboard to Canvas, Survey Respondents Want a User-friendly Learning System." *The Kent Stater.* https://kentstater.com/971 /uncategorized/from-blackboard-to-canvas-survey-respondents-want-a-user -friendly-learning-system/.

Remley, Dirk. 2015. *How the Brain Processes Multimodal Technical Instructions.* Baywood Technical Communication Series. 2nd ed. Routledge.

Remley, Dirk. 2017a. *Managerial Communication and the Brain.* Business Expert press.

Remley, Dirk. 2017b. *The Neuroscience of Multimodal Persuasive Messages: Persuading the Brain.* Routledge.

Remley, Dirk. 2019. *The Neuroscience of Rhetoric in Management: Compassionate Executive Communication.* Routledge.

Ricketts, Mitch. 2007. "The Use of Narratives in Safety and Health Communi- cation." Doctoral diss., Kansas State University.

Rook, Karen S. 1987. "Effects of Case History Versus Abstract Information on Health Attitudes and Behaviors." *Journal of Applied Social Psychology* 17: 533–53.

Saltmarshe, Ella. 2018. "Using Story to Change Systems." *Stanford Social Innovation Review,* February 20. https://ssir.org/articles/entry/using _story_to_change_systems.

Sandor, Krisztian, and Ekin Genç. 2022. "The Fall of Terra: A Timeline of the Meteoric Rise and Crash of UST and LUNA." *Coindesk*, June 1. https:// www.coindesk.com/learn/the-fall-of-terra-a-timeline-of-the-meteoric -rise-and-crash-of-ust-and-luna/.

Schmalzle, R., Frank Hacker, Britta Renner, Christopher J. Honey and Harald T. Schupp. 2013. Neural correlates of risk perception during real-life risk communication. *Journal of Neuroscience* 33 (25): 10340–10347.

Scholartrix. 2022. "Terra Founder Do Kwon Responds to Tax Evasion Charges in South Korea." May 23.

Scott, J. Blake. 2023. Risk Communication. In *Keywords in Technical and Professional Communication*, edited by Han Yu and Jonathan Beuhl. UP of Colorado.

Sheridan, David M., Jim Ridolfo, and Anthony J. Michel, eds. 2012. "The Available Means of Persuasion." In *Mapping a Theory and Pedagogy of Multimodal Public Rhetoric*. Parlor Press.

Shibu, Sherin. 2025. "'Difficult Decision': Amazon Announces a New Round of Layoffs. Here Are the Roles Affected." *Entrepreneur.* https://www .msn.com/en-us/money/companies/difficult-decision-amazon-announces -a-new-round-of-layoffs-here-are-the-roles-affected/ar-AA1y8ur6.

Shnurenko, George. 2018. "10 Bitcoin Millionaires—People Who Got Rich From Cryptocurrency." *UToday*, June 2. https://u.today/guides/blockchain /10-bitcoin-millionaires-people-who-got-rich-from-cryptocurrency.

Simons, Herbert W., and Jean G. Jones. 2011. *Persuasion and Society*. Routledge.

"SUNY Chancellor Announces 3-pronged Attack on Campus Covid." 2020. *The Buffalo News*, September 6.

South City Hospital. 2022. "South City Hospital Provides Notice of Data Privacy Incident."

Thorbecke, Catherine. 2022. "Amazon Confirms It has Begun Laying Off Employees." *CNN Business*, CNN.com. https://www.cnn.com/2022/11/16 /tech/amazon-layoffs.

Yahoo Finance. 2022. Bitcoin. https://finance.yahoo.com/quote/BTC-USD /history/.

Zak, Paul J. 2014. "Why Your Brain Loves Good Storytelling." *Harvard Business Review*, October 28. https://hbr.org/2014/10/why-your-brain-loves -good-storytelling.

Zak, Paul J. 2015. "Why Inspiring Stories Make Us React: The Neuroscience of Narrative." *Cerebrum*. https://pmc.ncbi.nlm.nih.gov/articles/PMC4445577/.

Zak, Paul J. 2017. "The Neuroscience of Trust." *Harvard Business Review*. https:// hbr.org/2017/01/the-neuroscience-of-trust.

About the Author

Dirk Remley is Professor of English at Kent State University where he teaches courses in technical and professional writing among other courses. He has authored several works linking neuroscience with rhetoric in technical and professional communication.

Index